PRAISE FOR

THE **RELATIONSHIP** ADVANTAGE

"In a world obsessed with shortcuts and hacks, *The Relationship Advantage* brings us back to what truly creates results: showing up consistently, adding value, and putting people first. This book lays out a practical, repeatable system for building relationships that compound over time. Anyone who wants a sustainable path to increased influence and opportunity should read it and learn from Barb Betts, who is a master."

—**Rory Vaden,** coauthor of the *New York Times* bestseller *Wealthy and Well-Known* and cofounder of Brand Builders Group

"Barb Betts proves that the most powerful way to connect is by showing up real, relatable, and fully human. If you want confidence that lasts and relationships that matter, this book is your new go-to."

—**Jen Gottlieb,** bestselling author of *Be Seen* and cofounder of Super Connector Media

"This is a must-read book for sales professionals. Barb Betts grounds us in the understanding that when we build relationships from a place of authentic connection and service, enduring partnerships emerge. This book offers compelling insights and practical ideas to help you understand how to build relationships that last a lifetime and reminds us all that life is people. Bravo!"

—**Ryan Estis,** global sales and leadership expert and coauthor of *Prepare for Impact*

"If you think 'networking' is swapping cards and chasing likes, read this. Barb shows you how to be seen, be human, and be useful . . . consistently. Her Relationship Operating System makes people feel known and valued, which is why the results keep compounding. This is how you build a legacy, not just a pipeline."

—**Frankie Russo,** eight-time Inc. 500 founder and bestselling author of *Breaking Why*

"In a world chasing algorithms and applause, Barb Betts reminds us that the real flex is connection. *The Relationship Advantage* is a master class in courage, authenticity, and the kind of leadership that starts with self-trust. This isn't networking—it's nourishment for the human spirit."

—**Judi Holler,** *USA Today* bestselling author of *Holler at Your Dreams*

"Barb Betts reminds us that connection isn't just good for business—it's good for the soul. *The Relationship Advantage* is a game-changing guide to building trust, deepening relationships, and leaving a legacy of genuine impact. This is the book every leader and human needs right now."

—**Erin King,** the "Energy Expert" and bestselling author of *You're Kind of a Big Deal*

"Authentic relationships are the foundation of every high-performing team—and this book nails it. It's inspirational, actionable, and exactly what leaders need in a world that's forgotten how to truly connect. A must-read for anyone who wants to elevate their game in any arena."

—**Alan Stein Jr.,** performance coach and bestselling author of *Raise Your Game* and *Next Play*

"Barb shows that connection is an act of kindness, and kindness is a form of leadership. *The Relationship Advantage* is a powerful invitation to lead with heart, treat people with dignity, and build a legacy of love and humanity."

—**Shola Richards,** bestselling author of *Civil Unity*

"Barb Betts has cracked the code on what most people miss. Your network isn't about who you know; it's about who trusts you enough to open doors you can't reach alone. This book is the playbook for turning genuine human connection into your most powerful competitive advantage."

—**AJ Vaden,** coauthor of the *New York Times* bestseller *Wealthy and Well-Known* and cofounder of Brand Builders Group

"This book feels like a deep exhale. *The Relationship Advantage* gives you practical tools to build trust online or offline and shows how people feel seen and valued. Whether you lead, sell, teach, or support clients, you'll find guidance that strengthens the way you connect with others. This book helps you show up with more presence and more awareness of how your relationships shape every part of your world."

—**Chelsea Peitz,** international keynote speaker and bestselling author

"Forget everything you think you know about leadership. Barb Betts just re-wrote the playbook. *The Relationship Advantage* isn't another leadership book. It's the missing manual for anyone who's ever wondered why some leaders build empires while others barely build compliance. This is the book that finally proves what the best leaders have always known: Relationships aren't a soft skill. They're *the* skill. Read it, live it, watch what happens."

—**Chris Dyer,** bestselling author of *The Power of Company Culture*

"Barb reminds us that the relationship we have with ourselves sets the tone for every connection we create. *The Relationship Advantage* is a beautiful invitation to be who you came to be—whole, present, and connected."

—**Tara Renze,** bestselling author of *Be Who You Came to Be*

"As someone who's spent a career helping leaders connect to others with intention and purpose, I can say this book is pure gold. It's the playbook for building relationships that outlast titles, quotas, and seasons. Read it, live it, and watch your world change, one winning Monday at a time."

—**Paul Epstein,** former NFL and NBA executive; two-time bestselling author; founder, WIN MONDAY™

"Barb Betts delivers a powerful reminder that relationships aren't a 'soft' skill—they're the competitive edge. *The Relationship Advantage* is a timely, practical guide to building trust, influence, and meaningful impact."

—**David Burkus,** author of *Best Team Ever*

"Barb Betts makes building relationships feel less like a chore and more like a superpower you can learn. This book is packed with simple, human insights that remind you that connection doesn't require perfection—just presence, curiosity, and a willingness to show up as yourself. Read it and watch your business—and referrals—skyrocket."

—**Brittany Hodak,** author of *Creating Superfans*

"If you want to create belonging, start here. Barb reminds us that belonging is built one authentic connection at a time."

—**Smiley Poswolsky,** author of *Friendship in the Age of Loneliness*

"Relationships are our most powerful resource, yet cultivating them requires systematic intention. Barb's book is full of practical systems and timeless wisdom anyone can implement. *The Relationship Advantage* is a master class in the forgotten art of being a good human. Everyone should read it!"

—**Eric Johnson,** CEO, Teamzy Inc., and author of *Power Hour Boss*

"I've had a front-row seat to Barb Betts's brilliance for years, and I'm thrilled she finally bottled it in this book. If you've ever wondered how some people naturally attract trust, loyalty, and opportunity—this is the playbook. Barb is the one who walks into a room and leaves with five new friends by lunch, and *The Relationship Advantage* shows you exactly how. It's smart, soulful, and full of real-world wisdom that turns genuine connection into unstoppable success."

—**Amy LaVallie,** lead personal brand strategist, Brand Builders Group

THE **RELATIONSHIP** ADVANTAGE

Unlock the Life-Changing Power of Human Connection

Barb Betts

www.amplifypublishinggroup.com

The Relationship Advantage: Unlock the Life-Changing Power of Human Connection

For more information, please contact:
Amplify Publishing, an imprint of Amplify Publishing Group
620 Herndon Parkway, Suite 220
Herndon, VA 20170
info@amplifypublishing.com

Library of Congress Control Number: 2025926043

CPSIA Code: PRV0126A

ISBN-13: 979-8-89138-983-0

Printed in the United States

To Harold, Chris, and Mandy.

The three of you are my life's most important relationships,
my constant reminder that success begins at home,
and the legacy I am most proud of.

CONTENTS

Introduction: Why This Book Had to Be Written xi

PART I: Your Relationship with Yourself

1. The Relationship That Changes Everything 3
2. Permission to Stop Hiding 19
3. Permission to Reframe Comparison 29
4. Permission to Embrace Self-Doubt 37
5. Permission to Forget People Pleasing 45

PART II: Your Relationship with Others

6. The Foundation: Making People Feel Seen, Known, and Important 57
7. Beyond Emotional Intelligence: The Power of Relational Intelligence 71
8. The VVR Factor: Visibility, Vulnerability, and Relatability in Action 83
9. Digital Relationships: From Screens to Real Connection 99
10. The Relationship Operating System: When Good Intentions Meet Strategic Action 119

PART III: Relationships That Make an Impact

11. Everyone's in Sales: The Powerful Truth About Influence 151
12. Leadership Through Connection: When Trust Becomes Your Greatest Currency 187
13. Building Communities, Not Just Networks 201
14. The Legacy You Leave—Living in the Dash 219

Acknowledgments 235
About the Author 237

INTRODUCTION

Why This Book Had to Be Written

I was the kid with the birthmark.

It was a port-wine stain, dark red and impossible to hide, and it was the very first thing people noticed about me. Long before I could even form a full sentence, I knew I was different. Not in the special, celebrated kind of way that gets you picked first or praised for standing out, but in the way that made other kids pause, whisper, or sometimes point. I didn't always understand what they were saying, but I could feel it. Kids don't need words to know when they're being looked at differently. I knew it in the awkward silences, the glances exchanged between parents, and the way some people looked past me as quickly as they could.

By the time I hit elementary school, I had a full collection of things that made me feel "less than." I was overweight, had big, thick glasses, metal braces, and the birthmark—my forever giveaway that I couldn't hide. I always felt like I took up too much space, but not the kind of space anyone was excited about. I wasn't the cute one. I wasn't the funny one. I wasn't the one getting invited to birthday parties or whispered about in a good way. I was the last girl invited to slumber parties, the last one picked for the kickball game. I was the girl who hoped no one would notice her walking in, who silently panicked every time teams were picked in PE class, and who tried to disappear during class presentations. The one who felt like she had to earn her place in every room.

And at home? I was alone a lot.

I was an only child, a latchkey kid before I even knew what that meant. During middle school and high school, I would wake up to an empty house. There was no breakfast ready on the table; there was only silence. I would find a ride to school or walk, and then I would walk home by myself and let myself into an empty house every afternoon. I figured out how to take care of myself. I would make myself a plate of Triscuits and cheddar cheese, turn on *The Oprah Winfrey Show*, and sit on the couch trying to pretend I wasn't lonely. There were no siblings running around, no parents waiting at the door to ask me how my day was.

Now, to be clear, my parents worked hard and did the best they could with what they had, but they worked outside of the home and had extremely long commutes, which meant they left early and weren't home until sometimes past dinnertime.

That silence did something to me. Yes, it taught me how to be self-sufficient, but it also left me aching. I craved connection. I wanted someone to ask how my day was. I wanted someone to choose me, to see me, to say, "You matter. I see who you are."

Because I didn't have that, I started trying to become it for other people.

I learned how to show up in ways that made people feel comfortable, even when I didn't feel that way myself. I became hyperaware of other people's moods, preferences, and needs. I could walk into a room and read the energy instantly. I knew who was uncomfortable, who was holding back, and who needed to feel included. And without realizing it, I started building relationships—not for strategy, not for sales, but because deep down, I never wanted anyone else to feel the way I had felt for so long: invisible.

That's where my gift was born.

Not in a boardroom. Not in a classroom. In the cafeteria. On the playground. On the walk home from school alone. My relational strength came from my personal ache. The way I knew how to make someone feel remembered wasn't something I read in a book; it was something I desperately needed growing up.

That girl—the one with the glasses, the braces, the quiet afternoons, and the tender heart—she still lives in me. And honestly? She's the reason I've been able to build everything I have.

Today, I've built multimillion-dollar businesses. I speak on stages. I train entrepreneurs, sales professionals, and leaders on how to grow their impact and income through relationships. I've built a life filled with people I love and people who love me back for who I truly am.

But none of it started with a fancy plan. It didn't come from cold-calling my way to the top. I didn't have a viral moment or a massive following that opened doors.

I didn't start with strategy; I started with heart.

I built my business one relationship at a time, rooted in trust.

And every step of the way, I led with what mattered most: care.

Relationships didn't just grow my business. They *are* my business. But more than that . . . they saved me. They showed me that I was never too much. That I wasn't broken. That being different didn't make me less; it made me real. And that realness? It's what people crave.

What Is a Relationship, Really?

Before we dive deeper into building authentic connections, let's get clear on what we're actually talking about. Most people think they know what a relationship is, but when you dig into the standard definition, it reveals why so many struggle to build meaningful ones.

According to *Merriam-Webster*, a relationship is "the way in which two or more concepts, objects, or people are connected, or the state of being connected." That's it. Technically, you have a "relationship" with your mail carrier, your grocery store cashier, and the person who cuts you off in traffic. The dictionary definition is so broad it's practically meaningless.

No wonder we're confused about relationships. By this definition, every interaction qualifies as a relationship, regardless of depth, trust, or mutual care. It's like saying a house and a mansion are both just "structures with walls and a roof." Technically true, but it's missing everything that actually matters.

Here's my definition of a relationship:

A relationship is a real, human connection grounded in authenticity, trust, and care.

Notice what this definition requires:

1. Authenticity—showing up as who you really are
2. Trust—built through consistent actions over time
3. Care—genuine concern for the other person's well-being

This isn't just about being connected—it's about being *meaningfully* connected.

This distinction matters because it changes how you approach every interaction. Instead of collecting connections like trading cards, you focus on cultivating relationships that actually enrich your life and the lives of others. Instead of networking to expand your contact list, you invest in building your trust account with people who matter.

The difference between a connection and a relationship is the difference between knowing someone's name and knowing their story. Between having their phone number and having their trust. Between being in their network and being in their life.

I'm sure you each have your own stories—feelings of loneliness or disconnection. And the fact that you're here means you deeply understand not only the importance of relationships in our personal and professional lives but also how deeply healing they can be.

This book is designed to give readers what they crave—a practical path toward building more meaningful, lasting relationships. Relationships are hard. By grounding our inherent desire to connect with others in clear strategies and relatable examples, the three sections of this book will help you move past the hesitation and overthinking that often hold relationships back.

The first section centers on the most important relationship you'll ever have: the one with yourself. Here, I unpack some of the most common barriers to authentic self-connection, from the struggle to be truly seen to the traps of comparison, negative self-talk, and people pleasing that pull us away from our true selves.

The second section turns outward, focusing on how we build and sustain relationships with others. It explores principles such as serving before asking, showing up with consistency, practicing emotional intelligence, embracing vulnerability, navigating digital relationships, and developing systems that make others feel genuinely valued while helping you stay organized and focused on where and who to put your energy toward.

Finally, the third section broadens the lens to consider the lasting impact of our relationships. You'll discover how the connections you nurture create ripples that shape lives—not just in the moment, but long after your presence is gone.

This isn't a book about strategy, although you'll find tons. It's not just about leadership, although it will make you a better leader. It's not even just about sales, though the sales results will blow your mind. This is a book about being human. About showing up not as a version of yourself you think people want but as the person you truly are.

If you've ever struggled with self-doubt . . .

If you've ever worked hard to be liked but still felt unseen . . .

If you've ever succeeded on the outside but felt empty on the inside . . .

If you've ever wondered if you're "too much" or "not enough" . . .

And if you've ever craved relationships that feel safe, real, and rooted in trust, not performance . . .

This book is for you.

I'm not here to teach you how to "work the room." I'm here to show you how to change the room through presence, through authenticity, and through real connection that leads to real trust.

Because people don't refer perfection. They refer realness.

They don't remember who followed the script. They remember who made them *feel something*.

And they don't stay loyal to someone who showed up once. They stay loyal to the one who kept showing up.

So wherever you are in your journey—whether you're in business, sales, or leadership, or just want more meaningful relationships in your life—I want to invite you to come a little closer.

This book is your permission slip to stop performing and start connecting.

To stop chasing and start choosing.

To stop hiding and finally be seen.

PART I

Your Relationship with Yourself

CHAPTER 1

The Relationship That Changes Everything

For as long as I can remember, I thought being good at something would make me feel good about myself. I thought if I could just do well, perform, produce, provide, and achieve, I'd earn the right to feel confident. That's what we're taught, right? Work hard, do a good job, get recognized, and finally feel secure. But no one tells you what happens when you do all those things and still feel unseen, unsure, and unvalued. When the outside looks polished, but the inside still questions its place in the room.

I built a successful business. I started my real estate business simply to help friends and family—like many agents do at the beginning—without expecting it to go much further. I quickly realized I had a knack for it, and before long, I had built a thriving, full-time career. As my business grew, I found myself juggling more than I could handle alone, so I brought on buyers' agents and assistants; eventually my husband even joined the team. Together, we built a team that evolved and expanded over time, eventually leading me to open my own brokerage. Along the way, I worked with a wide range of clients, from first-time homebuyers to multimillion-dollar properties.

From the outside, it looked like I had it all together. And I was proud of what I had built. I loved my work, I loved the people I served, and I genuinely believed in what I was doing. But still, there were moments—more than I ever admitted out loud—when I felt like I was performing. Like I was putting on the version of me the world wanted to see instead of the one who was quietly sitting behind it all, wondering, *Am I enough for this?*

It took me years to realize the truth. The problem wasn't the work. It wasn't the business or the strategy or the team. It was me. Or more specifically, it was the relationship I had with myself.

That's what this chapter is about. Because before we can talk about connecting with others, building trust, or deepening relationships in business or life, we have to start with the one person you are guaranteed to be in a relationship with every single day: yourself.

And if that relationship isn't solid, everything else will feel off. Even when it looks right.

The Mask We Don't Know We're Wearing

Growing up, I learned how to wear masks without even realizing I was doing it. As an only child and a latchkey kid, I got really good at independence. I figured things out on my own. I was the girl who knew how to take care of herself, make her own snack, and get her homework done without being asked. From a young age, I learned how to be capable. And that capability became a core part of how I found my worth.

What others praised as independence or maturity often felt, to me, like being asked to carry more than my share. I remember one particular weekend when I was about twelve. My parents were leaving for a bowling tournament, and my grandmother was supposed to come stay with me, but she couldn't get there until late Saturday night.

My mom was rushing around packing their bags and said, "Barb, Grandma won't be here until around ten p.m., so you'll need to handle dinner and getting yourself ready for bed. There's money on the counter for pizza, and you know where everything is."

My dad looked at me seriously and said, "Think you can manage on your own for a few hours? We're counting on you."

"Of course," I said, trying to sound confident. "I've got it."

When they got home Sunday evening, they found the house exactly as they'd left it—clean, organized, and me with my homework done, having handled the entire weekend without a single problem.

My mom looked around and said, "Barb, I don't know what we'd do without you. You just handle everything, don't you? You're like a little adult."

My dad nodded and added, "We never have to worry about you. You've got it all figured out. Most kids your age couldn't have managed all that."

They meant it as the highest compliment. And I beamed with pride. But underneath that smile, I was a twelve-year-old who had spent Saturday evening eating pizza alone, wondering if other kids my age were home by themselves, and trying not to think about how big and quiet the house felt until Grandma finally arrived.

What they saw was capability. What I felt was the pressure of always needing to be the one who "had it all figured out." Carrying that responsibility so young made me believe my value came from proving myself—again and again. And when you don't feel chosen, you start trying to earn your place.

You learn to be agreeable, helpful, funny, and likable. You become who people need you to be in order to feel safe in a room. You tune in to other people's needs before your own because, on some level, you've learned that *being needed* is the fastest route to *being wanted*.

I brought all of that into my adult life, into my work, and into my business. I knew how to read a room. I knew how to show up. I knew how to take care of others. But I didn't know how to take care of myself. I could advocate for a client like a champion, but when it came to advocating for myself, I would shrink. I could teach others how to speak confidently, but I still battled imposter syndrome in rooms full of successful people. I could pour into relationships, but I wasn't pouring into the one I had with myself.

That's what most people don't realize. The version of you who shows up at work every day isn't just a set of skills. It's a whole person. You bring your beliefs, your insecurities, your coping mechanisms, and your inner dialogue into every meeting, every sales conversation, and every leadership moment. And if the voice inside your head is one of doubt, criticism, or fear, no amount of external validation will make you feel like you belong.

The Truth About Authenticity

Let's talk about *authenticity*.

We love that word, don't we? It's everywhere. In every self-help book, in leadership keynotes, on inspirational quote cards, and all over Instagram. We tell people to "just be yourself" like it's the easiest advice in the world. But here's the truth: Authenticity is one of the most misunderstood concepts in both business and life.

Merriam-Webster defines authenticity as "being true to one's own personality, spirit, or character."* Sounds simple enough. But in a world where we are constantly being shaped by expectations, curated images, and the pressure to perform, being true to yourself isn't always

* *Merriam-Webster Unabridged*, s.v. "authenticity," accessed August 19, 2025, https://unabridged.merriam-webster.com/unabridged/authenticity.

straightforward. We've turned authenticity into a performance. We think it means sharing every thought in our head or throwing our life up on social media in the name of being "real."

Let me be clear: That's not authenticity. That's oversharing.

There's a dangerous myth about authenticity that needs to be addressed: the idea that being authentic means bringing your whole self to every situation. This isn't authenticity—it's poor judgment.

Authenticity doesn't mean sharing every thought, feeling, or struggle with everyone you meet. It doesn't mean being the same person in every context or dumping your personal issues on professional colleagues. That's not vulnerability—that's a lack of boundaries.

There is a difference between transparency and wisdom. It's okay to have a filter. It's okay to keep things sacred. Authenticity isn't about saying everything. It's about saying what matters.

And here's the problem with the way we talk about it. When we tell people to "just be authentic," it sounds like something you have to perform. It makes authenticity feel like an action, like you have to *do* something or *be* something in order to earn it. But that's not authenticity at all. That's pressure. That's performance.

Here's my definition of authenticity:

Authenticity isn't about *doing* anything—
it's about undoing everything that *isn't you.*

True authenticity requires emotional intelligence. It means bringing the real parts of yourself that are appropriate for the context and relationship. You're not performing or pretending to be someone else, but you are being thoughtful about which aspects of your authentic self to share.

For example:

- Your grief over a family loss is authentic, but sharing those raw emotions during a client presentation isn't appropriate.
- Your excitement about a personal achievement is genuine, but monopolizing a team meeting to discuss it shows poor judgment.
- Your political opinions are real, but bringing them into every professional conversation can damage relationships unnecessarily.

It's about dropping the act, taking off the mask, and dismantling the walls you built to protect yourself from being hurt, judged, or rejected. It's not about putting on more layers. It's about removing them. It's not about oversharing every detail of your life or every thought in your head—that's not vulnerability; that's noise. It's about being real with what you choose to reveal, rooted in honesty and intention. And that work? It's terrifying. It's beautiful. And it's the kind of freedom that changes everything.

Because the opposite of authenticity isn't dishonesty. It's performance. Most of us don't lie to each other. But we do perform. We show the version of ourselves we think will be accepted. The one that fits the room. The one that's polished, filtered, and strategic. The one that keeps us safe.

Who You Bring with You

When I say your relationship with yourself is the foundation for every other relationship in your life, I'm not being metaphorical. I mean it quite literally. You are the common denominator in every room you walk into, every conversation you have, and every connection you make. And if that person you bring with you is exhausted, insecure, disconnected, or performing, you will always hit a ceiling.

This is especially true in business. We often think the barrier to our next level is something external. A better strategy, a bigger audience, and a more polished pitch. But in my experience, the real barrier is almost always internal. It's the unresolved insecurity. The unspoken fear. The self-doubt we've become so used to living with, we don't even realize it's making decisions on our behalf.

And here's why it matters. According to a study by the Simmons University Institute for Inclusive Leadership, 93 percent of people believe authenticity is important in the workplace.* But more than that—71 percent of those who feel they can be authentic say they're more confident, 60 percent say they're more engaged, and 46 percent report being happier overall. That's not fluff. That's data-backed evidence that being real doesn't just feel good—it changes how we perform and how we connect.

When leaders and team members alike show up authentically, psychological safety rises. Harvard researcher Amy Edmondson's work shows that psychological safety—the belief that you can speak up, take risks, and be vulnerable without fear of punishment—directly boosts team innovation, learning, and performance.† You want stronger teams? More innovation? Deeper trust? It starts with authenticity.

And there's more. According to a Brand Builders Group national research study on personal branding, 74 percent of Americans are more

---

* Simmons University Institute for Inclusive Leadership, *The Importance of Authenticity in the Workplace*, July 2021, https://www.inclusiveleadership.com/wp-content/uploads/2021/07/The-Importance-of-Authenticity-in-the-Workplace.pdf.

† Amy C. Edmondson, *The Fearless Organization: Creating Psychological Safety in the Workplace for Learning, Innovation, and Growth* (John Wiley & Sons, 2019).

likely to trust someone who has an established personal brand.* And what fuels a strong personal brand? Authenticity. People want to know the person behind the expertise. They want to connect with someone who feels real, not rehearsed. Authenticity doesn't just build trust—it builds influence, loyalty, and long-term impact.

The science backs this up in the most comprehensive way possible. And it's not just theoretical—decades of data show us that authentic relationships don't just improve how we feel; they improve how we live. The Harvard Grant Study has tracked over seven hundred individuals for more than eighty years, analyzing everything from career satisfaction to health, showing us what truly leads to a fulfilling, successful life.

The result? Strong, trusting relationships—especially with ourselves—are the single most significant factor in our happiness, health, and longevity.† It wasn't wealth, career, or even physical health that predicted life satisfaction at age eighty. It was the quality of relationships we built along the way.

Dr. Robert Waldinger, the study's current director, puts it this way: "The people who were the most satisfied in their relationships at age fifty were the healthiest at age eighty." It wasn't about their cholesterol levels at fifty, their career success, or their bank account balance. It was the quality of their relationships.

The study revealed that people with strong social connections live longer, have better physical health and sharper mental function, and report higher levels of life satisfaction. Meanwhile, loneliness was found to be as damaging to health as smoking or obesity.

---

* Brand Builders Group, *Trends in Personal Branding*, 2021, https://brandbuildersgroup.com/study/.

† Liz Mineo, "Over Nearly 80 Years, Harvard Study Has Been Showing How to Live a Healthy and Happy Life," *Harvard Gazette*, April 11, 2017, https://news.harvard.edu/gazette/story/2017/04/over-nearly-80-years-harvard-study-has-been-showing-how-to-live-a-healthy-and-happy-life/.

But here's what struck me most about these findings: The relationships that mattered weren't necessarily the most numerous ones. Quality trumped quantity every time. It wasn't about having hundreds of Facebook friends or maintaining massive networks. It was about having relationships characterized by trust, vulnerability, and genuine care—the same elements we've been talking about.

This eighty-year study confirms what I learned the hard way: The relationship you have with yourself sets the foundation for every other relationship in your life. And those relationships—built on authenticity, trust, and genuine connection—aren't just nice to have. They're literally what determine whether you'll live a long, healthy, and happy life.

Relationships Are Mirrors: You Can Only Build What You Can See

Here's a truth that most relationship advice ignores: You can only build relationships with others to the capacity that you see yourself. Your external relationships are mirrors of your internal relationship with yourself.

If you don't believe you're worthy of deep, meaningful connections, you'll unconsciously sabotage them when they start to develop. If you see yourself as fundamentally flawed or unlovable, you'll either attract people who confirm that belief or push away those who challenge it.

This isn't pop psychology—it's practical reality. The person who doesn't trust themselves struggles to trust others. The person who's constantly critical of themselves becomes critical in relationships. The person who doesn't value their own worth accepts treatment that reflects that low valuation.

Think of it as a self-worth ceiling. You might be able to build relationships that reach that ceiling, but you'll struggle to sustain anything that goes beyond what you believe you deserve. When someone offers you more trust, respect, or care than you think you're worth, it feels uncomfortable, unnatural, and even suspicious.

I've watched this play out countless times . . . including in myself. The talented professional who can't understand why they keep attracting demanding, boundary-crossing clients—until they realize they don't believe they deserve better treatment. The leader who wonders why their team doesn't trust them with important decisions—until they acknowledge they don't trust their own judgment.

The encouraging news is that this mirror effect works both ways. As you develop a healthier relationship with yourself—as you practice self-compassion, set appropriate boundaries, and honor your own worth—your capacity for healthy relationships with others expands naturally.

When you believe you deserve respect, you stop accepting disrespectful treatment. When you trust your own judgment, you can trust others more freely. When you're comfortable with your imperfections, you give others permission to be imperfect too.

This is why the first section of this book focuses on your relationship with yourself. You can't give what you don't have. You can't offer trust from an empty well or build confidence in others when you lack it yourself.

The Turning Point

It was a Thursday evening in late September, around 6:30 p.m. I had just finished my third closing of the month—what should have been a celebration. My clients were thrilled with their new home, and from the outside, I was crushing it.

I was sitting in my Chevy Suburban in the parking lot of the escrow office, engine still running, air conditioning humming against the lingering heat of the day. I should have been calling Harold to share the good news. I should have been planning how to celebrate another successful month. Instead, I was staring at the commission check in my hands, feeling absolutely nothing.

The closing had gone smoothly; there was no last-minute drama, no financing hiccups, and no inspection surprises. The kind of seamless transaction that agents dream about. My clients had hugged me, taken photos, and promised to refer me to everyone they knew. I had smiled and celebrated with them, playing the part of the successful agent who had just helped make their homeownership dreams come true.

But the moment I walked out of that building and got into my car, the performance stopped. What was left underneath was a hollow, disconnected feeling I couldn't shake. Sitting there alone in my car, face hot with tears and heart heavy with something I couldn't quite name, I realized that something had to change. I didn't need to change my work. I needed to change how I treated myself *inside the work*.

I had to learn to show up for myself the way I showed up for my clients. To be my own biggest advocate. To speak to myself with the same kindness I offered them when they were having a rough day. To set boundaries around my time and energy instead of saying yes to every request. To take breaks without guilt, to eat lunch instead of working through it, and to stop checking emails at 10:00 p.m. because I was afraid I might miss something urgent.

Most importantly, I had to stop tying my self-worth to my production numbers. When I had a slow month, I reminded myself that my value as a person wasn't determined by my commission check. When a deal fell through, I practiced treating myself with the same compassion I'd offer a friend facing disappointment. I started celebrating small wins—not just the big closings, but the meaningful conversations, the problems I solved, and the clients who felt heard and supported.

I also had to get honest about the voice in my head. For years, I had been my own harshest critic, replaying every mistake and questioning every decision. I started paying attention to my internal dialogue and asking, *Would I talk to a client this way?* The answer was always *no*. So I began the slow work of changing that conversation, treating myself like someone I actually cared about instead of someone I was trying to manage or control.

It wasn't an overnight shift. It was a journey, one of unlearning old habits, shedding layers of perfectionism, and stepping into a relationship with myself that was based on love, patience, and fierce care.

As I began to prioritize that relationship, everything else started to shift. The work still mattered, but it wasn't my identity anymore. I began to find peace in the in-between moments, joy in the small wins, and confidence that came from within, not just from what I accomplished.

That's when I truly started to thrive.

We all have what I call "armor." The personas we wear to protect our most tender places. For some people, it's confidence. For others, it's humor. For me, it was capability. I knew how to handle things. I knew how to get stuff done. I was the fixer. The one people could count on. And while being capable isn't a bad thing, it became my shield. As long as I was performing well, no one would question whether I was struggling inside. Not even me.

The turning point came when I realized the mask was getting in the way. I was craving deeper relationships. I wanted to feel seen. Known. Loved for who I was, not what I did. But I couldn't ask people to see me if I wasn't willing to let them. I had to let down the walls.

So when people told me to "just be myself," I didn't even know who that was. Because when you've spent years curating your image to be acceptable, likable, impressive, or in control, being yourself doesn't feel simple. It feels risky. We talk about authenticity like it's a trait—something you're either good at or not.

But it's not a trait. It's a practice. It's a choice. It's a commitment to show up as the truest version of you, even when it's messy. Especially when it's messy.

The Practice of Authenticity

You can't perform authenticity. You have to live it. You have to know who you are beneath the labels (like "Mom" or "Dad"), job titles, social media presence, and achievements. You have to understand your values, your wounds, your strengths, and your story. You have to get curious about the parts of yourself you've tried to hide or downplay. Because you can't build real relationships with other people if the relationship you have with yourself is based on pretending.

The truth is, you can't have an authentic relationship with anyone else until you have one with yourself.

You can't create trust when you don't trust your own voice. You can't make people feel seen when you refuse to look at your own truth.

Authenticity doesn't happen overnight. It's not a light switch you flip or a one-time decision you make. It's a practice. A process. A lifelong commitment to return to yourself over and over again. Some days, you'll feel aligned and grounded. Other days, the pressure to perform will sneak back in. That's normal. That's human. The goal isn't perfection—it's awareness. The work of being authentic is never really done, because the more you grow, the more you'll discover about who you truly are. And each version deserves your full presence.

Authenticity isn't about being perfect. It's about being true. And sometimes that truth is messy. It's emotional. It's uncomfortable. But it's also magnetic. People are drawn to what's real. They trust it. They connect to it. Not because it's polished, but because it's honest. Especially in business.

When I finally started showing up more honestly in my business—when I stopped scripting every word and just started speaking from the heart—everything shifted. Clients trusted me faster. Conversations got deeper. Referrals increased. Why? Because people could feel the difference. They weren't just buying a service. They were entering a relationship. And people don't build lasting relationships with your highlight reel. They build them with *you*.

You don't have to be perfect to be powerful. You don't have to be fearless to lead. You don't have to have it all figured out to make a real impact. You just have to be you. But not the version of you that you think the world wants. The *real* you. The one beneath the layers. The one who knows what matters. The one who has nothing to prove.

So how do you get there? You start by noticing when you're performing. When you're shrinking. When you're overexplaining. When you're filtering. You notice the moments that make you feel like you need to impress or please. And you get curious. Ask yourself, *Who am I trying to protect? What am I afraid they'll see? What story am I telling myself about what it takes to belong here?*

And then—gently, bravely—you challenge that story. You let your guard down, just a little. You say the honest thing. You ask the real question. You show up imperfectly but fully.

I didn't have the answers that day in my car. But I decided. I decided to stop performing and start paying attention. I started asking better questions. I started listening to the quiet parts of me I had ignored for too long.

That moment didn't fix everything, but it woke me up. It showed me that the most important work I would ever do wasn't building a business—it was rebuilding the relationship I had with myself.

This Is Where We Begin

This chapter is the foundation of everything else we will explore together in this book. We are going to talk about building relationships with others, with your business, with your clients, and with your community. But we cannot go there until we go here.

Because no matter what your role is—whether you are in sales, leadership, entrepreneurship, or simply navigating life—the person you bring with you matters more than any strategy you implement. And if you don't know, trust, or care for that person, nothing else will work the way you want it to.

Your confidence does not come from performance. It comes from permission. Permission to show up as your full self. Permission to stop pretending. Permission to let go of who you think you have to be so you can become who you actually are.

This is the relationship that changes everything. And the beautiful part is, you don't have to earn it. You just have to return to it.

We are so used to striving, achieving, and fixing. But this isn't about fixing anything. It's about remembering. It's about reconnecting with the version of you who is already worthy, already whole, and already enough.

So if you have spent years proving yourself . . .

If you have checked every box and still don't feel fulfilled . . .

If you have climbed the ladder and wondered why it still doesn't feel like you have arrived . . .

I want to tell you something I wish someone had told me.

You don't have to do more.

You just have to know yourself better.

And treat that relationship as the foundation for everything else you want to build.

That's where the magic begins. Because the truth is we're all craving permission. Permission to stop hiding. Permission to stop comparing. Permission to stop pretending that self-doubt means you don't belong. In the next chapters, we're going to talk about each of those things—one at a time. Because the more you understand them, the more power you'll have to release them. And when you do, you don't just become more authentic—you become unstoppable.

That's what we are doing here. And we are starting right where it matters most: with you.

CHAPTER 2

Permission to Stop Hiding

You weren't born afraid to be seen. You were born bald and naked. You came into this world unapologetically loud, unfiltered, and fully present. You didn't ask for permission to cry. You didn't apologize for needing to be held. You didn't worry if your thighs were too thick or if someone thought you were too much. You just were.

And then slowly, without realizing it, you learned to hide.

It didn't happen all at once. It never does. It starts small. Maybe someone laughed when you danced too freely. Maybe a teacher made you feel wrong for having a strong opinion. Maybe you were told you were too loud, too sensitive, or too much. So you adjusted. You pulled back. You smiled when you wanted to speak up. You tucked away the wildest parts of yourself in exchange for safety.

I know the feeling. I know it intimately. Because I spent years hiding too.

For me, it started with my hair. Or rather, the slow and painful process of losing it. I wasn't just someone who had hair. I was *known* for my hair. Thick, dark brown, curly. It was one of the first things people noticed about me growing up. It was part of my identity. It made me feel beautiful, confident, and powerful. Until one day, it started to vanish.

In my mid-thirties, I remember waking up one morning, brushing my hair, and finding two perfectly round bald spots, each the size of a fifty-cent piece, staring back at me in the mirror. I froze. They hadn't been there the day before. The hair was just . . . gone. The spots were smooth and bare and terrifying. I ran to my pillow, feverishly looking for my hair. Immediately all kinds of awful things went through my head. *I have cancer. I'm going bald. What if* all *my hair falls out?*

That day, I walked into the dance studio where I was teaching, and Miss Donna was sitting in the office. I always loved those few minutes before class started where we would just chat. Miss Donna was my first dance teacher when I was just a little girl and turned into a mentor for most of my adult life. She saw the look on my face, took one glance at the spots on my head, and gently said, "It's likely alopecia. It's probably autoimmune."

I had never even heard the word before. *Alopecia?* I was completely distracted in class that day. Every time I went to change the music on my phone to practice a routine, I'd sneak into Google and type things in like "sudden hair loss," "alopecia spots," and "do you die from alopecia?"

It then launched a medical journey.

Hiding Myself, Burying My Confidence

I saw doctors, specialists, and dermatologists. We discovered I had Hashimoto's, an autoimmune thyroid condition. But even with a diagnosis, no doctor could tell me what was going to happen next. No one could say how much hair I would lose or if it would grow back or when.

So I tried everything. And I mean *everything*. I spent thousands of dollars on shampoos, serums, vitamins, and promises-in-a-bottle. And then came the platelet-rich plasma (PRP) injections—these painful treatments were injected directly into my scalp. If you are sitting here wondering how painful that is, well, it's next level. But at that point I would've done *anything* to get my hair to grow back. I sat in the chair, trying to stay hopeful while they injected my head over and over again, hoping that this time it would work.

And sometimes, it did. The hair would grow back. Just enough to give me hope. And then it would fall out again.

Grow. Fall out. Grow. Fall out.

Like a heartbreaking cycle of hope and disappointment that never ended. Every day felt like a game of emotional roulette. I would wake up and wonder, *How much hair will be left today?* It didn't take long for the emotional weight to set in. It went on like this for over a decade. Grief. Shame. Fear. I found myself scanning every woman I passed, jealous of their thick ponytails, their effortless updos, and their full blowouts. Even my own husband, who has a head of thick, beautiful hair, took longer to blow-dry his than I did. That hurt in ways I couldn't even explain. It felt like the universe was mocking me.

I became a master of disguise. I learned how to use a product called Toppik—a powder made of colored keratin fibers that helps cover thinning hair and bald spots. It was my security blanket for years. I changed my part daily. I avoided lighting that could expose my scalp. I avoided drizzling rain like it was a thunderstorm for fear the powder would run down my face. I held my head at unnatural angles in conversations so people wouldn't catch a glimpse of the truth. I prayed that the flash from the camera wouldn't expose what I was trying so hard to hide.

That truth? I was hiding. I was hiding behind products, behind smiles, behind a carefully crafted version of myself that said, "I've got it together." That mask I learned to wear as a child—always capable, always handling things on my own—had carried into adulthood. I rarely asked for the support I deserved or needed, because I'd been conditioned to believe that showing vulnerability was somehow a failure.

One of the lowest points came after another failed PRP cycle; my dermatologist, who was doing the treatments, said, "It's not working. I can't keep charging you for this."

So I made an appointment with a hair transplant surgeon, desperate for a permanent solution. I walked in with my amazing husband, clinging to hope. Maybe, just maybe, this time I would hear what I wanted.

Instead, I sat across from a gentle doctor who looked me in the eyes and said, "Barb, you have three strikes in the hair department. All of our hair is programmed to fall out at a certain point in our lives. And yours is programmed to fall out now. It's not coming back."

The room felt still around me. His words hung heavy, sinking deep. A lump formed in my throat. I wanted to scream, to argue, to deny it—but there was nothing left to fight. It felt like the ground beneath me had cracked wide open.

I remember sitting silently in the car afterward, my hands resting in my lap, staring blankly through the windshield. The finality of it hit me like a wave. I didn't just lose hair that day. I lost a piece of my identity. But something else stirred beneath the grief: the smallest flicker of surrender. Maybe this wasn't something I was meant to keep fighting.

And so, a few weeks later, I made one of the scariest decisions of my life. I decided to make an appointment with a human hair company, Follea by Daniel Alain, for a consultation. I brought my daughter Mandy with me. She was twenty at the time, and just her being with me and walking beside me felt like a lifeline. I didn't know what to expect. I was afraid, anxious, and embarrassed. *Would I look fake? Would I feel like myself? Would I ever feel normal again?*

Now, I originally went in to look at hair toppers; they are full-length extensions that cover the entire top of your head and hang over your bio hair. I will never forget when Ashley, my consultant, examined my scalp and gently shook her head. "Barb," she said, "I don't think you are a candidate for a topper. You don't have enough bio hair to hold the clips in. I think you should try on a wig."

I looked at her like she had three heads and foam coming out of her mouth. "A wig? Absolutely not," I uttered. Wigs look fake. There's a stigma behind wigs. I am too *young* to wear a wig. I must have looked horrified, because Ashley stayed quiet. And then Mandy, my brave, brilliant daughter, looked at me and said, "Mom, do you know how many women wear full extensions? You just need help in a different area. I think you should try on the wig."

That moment cracked me wide open. I tried on a wig. And I cried.

I will never forget the moment I looked into the mirror. I hadn't felt beautiful in a long, long time.

I ended up ordering the hair, and then I made an even more courageous decision. I decided to share my story publicly on social media for the first time. I shared it all—my truth, my pain, the journey, and the letting go. I held nothing back. And I expected judgment.

But what I received was love. The messages poured in. People thanked me for going first. Women and men opened up about their own hiding. Addictions. Eating disorders. Grief. Shame. Things they'd never told anyone. They told me that my vulnerability made them brave.

But what happened to me—well, it changed my life!

Our business grew. More clients, more connections. I got invited onto stages I had only dreamed of. I was more visible and more real than ever before. And people responded to that. Because when you stop hiding, you don't just free yourself. You give others permission to do the same.

This was the true shift. I realized that I was confident. I was authentic. I was incredible. And the way I showed up—the real me—had an impact. As my mentor Rory Vaden says, "You are most powerfully positioned to serve the person you once were." I understood then that

I could reach the unconfident, inauthentic, people pleasing version of myself—the person I had been—and help others transform their lives and businesses in the same way.

My friends started saying things like, "Barb, you are so much more confident now." I'd respond by saying that the wig didn't make me confident. It revealed the confidence that had been buried beneath shame and struggle and self-protection. It wasn't just my hair I had been hiding. It was me.

Visibility Is a Choice

For years, I had been holding back the most authentic, brilliant parts of myself. The confident one. The smart one. The connector. The problem solver. The bright light. The real Barb. I'd been shrinking all of it because I was afraid it would be "too much."

Now, I show up differently. In business. In life. Onstage. I believe in myself. I trust my voice. I know that the right people will be drawn to the real me. I no longer need to pretend.

The old Barb would never have gone live on social media with no hair and no makeup. But I have. And I will again. Because I am no longer hiding. You don't have to hide either.

What part of you are you still tucking away? Is it your voice? Your dreams? Your softness? Your story?

Hiding might feel safe. But it comes at a cost, a cost that slowly chips away at your confidence, your joy, and your potential.

What I've learned is this: Hiding who you are doesn't just protect you; it holds you back from becoming everything you're capable of.

When you hide who you are, you limit who you can become.

And hiding doesn't always look like physical concealment. It can be silencing your story. Dimming your light. Minimizing your ideas.

Downplaying your opinions. It can be pretending you're fine when you're breaking inside.

Small Shifts to Start Showing Up

Close your eyes for a moment. Take a few deep breaths and clear your mind.

Think about the following questions: What parts of your physical body have you been hiding? What part of your personality have you been taught to be ashamed of? What part of yourself do only a few people really know? And what has hiding or covering up that part cost you?

Hiding is sneaky. It wears different masks. You may not even realize you're doing it. Here's how you might be hiding without noticing:

- You constantly second-guess yourself before speaking.
- You tone down your excitement so you won't seem "too much."
- You filter your photos and your life for approval.
- You say "yes" when you mean "no."
- You stay busy to avoid stillness with yourself.
- You downplay your accomplishments so others won't feel uncomfortable.
- You keep your dreams secret; you're afraid they'll sound unrealistic.
- You mirror other people's energy to feel accepted.
- You avoid vulnerability, even with people you love.
- You tell people what they want to hear instead of what you really think.
- You carry the weight of others' expectations instead of honoring your truth.
- You hide your feelings behind humor or sarcasm.

If you see yourself in even one of those, it's okay. This isn't about shame or judgment. It's about awareness—and awareness is where transformation begins.

Change doesn't have to be big or immediate. It starts with small, brave steps. So here are a few simple actions you can take to stop hiding and start showing up more fully:

- Speak up in that meeting where you usually stay quiet.
- Post the story you've been holding on to.
- Stop editing your personality to make others comfortable.
- Take and post the selfie without the filter.
- Ask for what you need, unapologetically.
- Tell the truth, your full truth, to one person you trust.

Remember, each small step forward is a victory. You don't have to do it all at once. The journey to being seen and known starts with showing up for yourself, even in the smallest ways.

The truth is you have to allow yourself to be seen. Not the curated version of you. Not the one who's perfectly polished and always put together. But the real you. The bright, bold, brilliant version who's been waiting for your permission.

Let that person show up. Let them speak. Let them take up space.

You weren't born afraid to be seen. You were taught that standing out was risky.

Now it's time to unlearn that belief and return to who you've always been.

The truth is we don't become invisible because we've aged or changed; we become invisible because we've been hiding for too long. The more we disconnect from who we truly are, the more we fade from our own lives. But here's the good news: Visibility is a choice, and it's one you can make right now.

You don't have to shrink to fit into spaces that were never meant for you. You don't have to water yourself down so others can feel more comfortable. That was survival. But now? Now it's time for expansion.

When was the last time you asked yourself, *How do I really feel?* When was the last time you showed up without a filter, without a mask? When was the last time you let someone else really see you? When was the last time you saw yourself?

Sometimes we don't even realize we're hiding. We just know we don't feel alive or fulfilled or connected anymore. But once you become aware of how you've been disconnecting from your true self, you can begin the work of coming back.

Think back to the moment you stopped raising your hand. The first time you quieted your opinion to keep the peace. The season when you stopped asking for more because someone made you feel like your dreams were too big.

This is your moment to reclaim it.

Don't wait to feel ready. Don't wait until it's perfect. The path to becoming visible begins with one courageous decision: to be seen, just as you are.

And you are already enough.

CHAPTER 3

Permission to Reframe Comparison

I was sitting near the back of the ballroom at a real estate conference in 2019, my legs crossed, notebook resting in my lap, heart buzzing with anticipation. At that point in my journey, I had started dipping my toe into speaking. I had delivered sessions at real estate events, facilitated trainings, and stood in front of rooms full of professionals, but I was still in the early stages. I hadn't yet found my rhythm or my voice.

Teaching had always been my dream—long before real estate, before sales, before business. I wanted to be a teacher my whole life. There was something about standing in front of a group, sharing knowledge, inspiring growth, and lighting a spark in others that felt like purpose. Yet here I was, standing at the edge of that dream in a new form—public speaking—wondering if I had what it took to leap into a bigger world: bigger stages, bigger audiences, bigger impact.

Then Kindra Hall walked onto the stage.

She wasn't flashy. She didn't need to be. She carried herself with a calm confidence that was almost magnetic. The moment she opened her mouth, the room shifted. It was like every person leaned in just a little bit more. She spoke with purpose but also with ease. Her timing was impeccable, her humor perfectly placed. She told stories that weren't just relevant—they were unforgettable. And the way she carried herself? It was like the stage belonged to her.

And there I sat at the back of the room, watching her unfold a dream I had quietly held in my heart. I wasn't just admiring her skill; I was feeling something deeper. Something quieter. Something heavier. It was a mix of awe and doubt, a blend of inspiration laced with insecurity. A voice whispered inside me, a voice I've known for years but still struggle to silence: *You're not there. And maybe . . . you never will be.*

At the time, I didn't have the language to name it. But looking back, it's clear as day: I was comparing my chapter one to her chapter thirteen.

That moment has stayed with me, not because of what it told me about Kindra, but because of what it revealed about me. About how easily I could be pulled away from my truth, my dream, when I let someone else's success rewrite the narrative of my own worth.

Comparison Is the Thief of Authenticity

Comparison doesn't announce itself loudly. It creeps in through admiration. It disguises itself as ambition. But it has a sharp edge, one that cuts our confidence and corrodes our authenticity. And that's the part that's most dangerous. Because comparison doesn't just make you feel behind. It makes you question who you are.

Over time, something in me began to shift. I stopped seeing Kindra as a measuring stick and started seeing her as a map. She was doing something I wanted to do, yes, but instead of letting that diminish me, I began to get curious. What could I learn from her? What did her path show me was possible? I knew she had support groups and communities, so I found my own keynote support community. I paid attention to her story. She had a book. Could I write one too? She had a speaking coach. Maybe that's something I needed. She wasn't just proof of what I wasn't; she was an example of what I *could* become, a path to what is possible.

And that's the thing comparison never tells you: The people who inspire you most might not be ahead of you to make you feel behind. They might be there to show you the path.

But social media does not help. If anything, it fuels the fire. In my sales career, especially in real estate, I've seen comparison become a full-time sport. Real estate, in particular, is one of the most image-driven, numbers-obsessed industries you can be in. The awards, the production levels, the top-tier agent badges. Every time you log on, someone is celebrating a six-figure month or posing with their latest Just Sold sign.

And I'm all for celebrating wins. But the constant highlight reel can be exhausting. Because it's so easy to start measuring your value by someone else's metrics. So easy to forget that you're not seeing the full story. So it's easy to start thinking, *I'm not doing enough*, when the truth is, you're just doing something different; you are just on a different path.

Over the years, I've had to teach myself this: I don't know their goals. I don't know their story. I don't know if they're willing to miss their kid's 3:00 p.m. baseball game to chase a deal, or if they've structured their life differently. Maybe they don't prioritize their daughter's dance competition weekends like I did. Maybe they don't have a family to juggle. Maybe they have different values. Maybe they're in a different season.

That's what we forget in comparison. Context.

And nowhere is that more brutal than in parenting.

I can't even begin to count the number of times I've stood in the school pickup line and seen a mom show up with her makeup perfectly done, her hair curled, a handcrafted snack in hand, and matching outfits on her kids, and I've thought, *How is she doing it all?* Meanwhile, I'm in my car with my hair in a messy bun, fielding work calls and silently praying that I remembered to put a note in my kids' lunchboxes.

But what I've come to believe, what I know to be true, is that effortlessness is often an illusion. That mom? Maybe she was up at 4:00 a.m. Maybe she cried in the car. Maybe she's drowning in her own comparison game, just like me. We never know what someone else is carrying. And yet we compare ourselves to a version of them that may not even be real.

That's why I say this with my whole heart: **Comparison is the thief of authenticity.**

Not because it makes us jealous, but because it makes us forget ourselves.

Stop Shrinking, Start Stretching

Even as I've grown in the speaking world, I've had moments when comparison tried to creep in. When I joined Brand Builders Group, I met Brittany Hodak, and to be honest, I had a moment of panic and sheer doubt. Here was this amazing woman, speaking on similar topics, with similar values, already landing the gigs I dreamed of. And for a second, I wondered if there was room for both of us.

But that couldn't have been further from the truth. Her success didn't take anything away from me. In fact, it expanded what I believed was possible. We weren't duplicates. We were different. Both needed. Both worthy.

So what changed? I stopped letting comparison shrink me. And I started letting curiosity stretch me.

Many who study the laws of the universe observe that when someone close to you is achieving or experiencing something you desire, it can actually be a sign that your goal is about to manifest. Seeing aspects of your intention reflected in the actions, conversations, or opportunities around you is an external indicator that your focus and effort are aligning with the outcome you want.

I began to believe, deeply, that if she could do it, so could I. Not her way. My way. And the most powerful mindset shift of all? I stopped asking, *Why not me?* from a place of defeat and started asking it from a place of belief.

Why not me? Why not now? Why not this voice, this message, this story?

And if you're stuck in comparison right now, I want you to hear me: You're not behind. You're not failing. You're not missing some magical quality that everyone else seems to have. You are in a season that no one else can fully understand. You have values no one else can define. And you have a story no one else can tell. So I have to ask you, WHY NOT YOU?

Comparison will try to convince you that the only way to matter is to become like someone else. But the truth is, the only way to truly make an impact is to be more of *yourself*.

Kindra wasn't my competition. And neither was Brittany. They were an inspiration. A reminder. A clue. They reminded me that it's possible. And that possibility lives in me, too.

Let other people's success inspire you, but never let it erase you. Use it as a compass. Let it lead you deeper into your own growth. Because while the world is full of voices, it has never heard yours the way you're about to share it.

And that, my friend, is more than enough.

Actions to Reframe Comparison with Curiosity

1. **Name the Comparison Out Loud**

The next time you catch yourself comparing, pause and say (or write):

> "I'm comparing right now, and that's okay."

Awareness is the first step to shifting out of it. Naming the moment disarms the shame.

2. **Ask a Curiosity Question**

Instead of spiraling into *Why not me?* from a place of lack, ask:

> "What is this showing me about what I want?"

Use their success as a mirror to your own desires—not a measure of your worth.

3. **Separate the Season**

Write down three truths about your current life season.
Are you raising kids? Caring for someone? Building slowly on purpose?

Remind yourself: Different seasons call for different priorities.

4. **Celebrate Someone Who Triggers You**

When you feel comparison creeping in, flip the script. Send that person a note, comment, or message and celebrate them:

> "You inspired me today. Thank you."

It shifts you from competition to connection.

5. Reaffirm Your Path

Write this down and say it out loud:

There is no one else like me.
I don't need to be ahead—I just need to be aligned.

Repeat this whenever comparison makes you question your enoughness.

Comparison will always be there trying to pull you back, but now you have tools to meet it differently. Remember, this journey isn't about perfection; it's about progress. Every time you catch yourself comparing and choose curiosity instead, you're stepping closer to your authentic self.

Keep showing up. Keep believing in your unique path. Your voice matters, your story matters, and the world is waiting to hear it—exactly as only you can tell it.

CHAPTER 4

Permission to Embrace Self-Doubt

It was ten years ago, and I was attending my very first Legislative Day for the California Association of REALTORS® in Sacramento. I had just stepped into my role as a new director at my local association, and this trip felt way above my pay grade.

That morning, I sat in the room for the briefing, getting all the information we would discuss with our elected officials later that day. I didn't understand the process. I didn't know the talking points. I barely knew the names of the key legislators, let alone how to confidently advocate for policy change. I had never done anything like this before.

Everyone else in the room looked like they belonged there. They carried themselves with certainty, nodding at the presentation, flipping through briefing packets, and talking about upcoming meetings with lawmakers like it was just another Tuesday. I was sitting in a folding chair inside the Sacramento Convention Center, already feeling like the biggest outsider in the room.

And then my phone buzzed.

It was a text from our CEO, Phil Hawkins, someone I admired deeply. It said:

"Barb, meet us at the back of the room in five minutes. We're taking you with us to a private meeting with Assemblymember Tom Daly."

My stomach dropped.

Assemblymember Tom Daly? A private meeting?

My first thought wasn't excitement; it was complete panic. I thought, *Why me?* Followed quickly by, *They're going to find out I have no idea what I'm doing.*

I was being invited into a room I didn't feel ready for. A room filled with power, policy, and presence. And every insecure part of me rose to the surface; they were all screaming.

You don't belong! You're not ready! You're not enough!

I made my way to the back of the room, palms sweating, heart racing, trying to steady my breathing and silence the spiraling thoughts in my head. The hallway leading out of the convention center felt long and loud, every step echoing with doubt.

Do It Anyway

Phil greeted me with a smile, completely calm, as if this invitation to meet with a state assemblymember was no big deal. But to me it felt *monumental*. He didn't explain much, just said, "You're coming with us." And I did, mostly because I respected him so deeply, and partly because I didn't have time to think of a reason to say no or find an escape route.

But as we started walking toward the capitol building, I felt the weight of that invitation. It wasn't just a meeting. It was a moment.

We didn't end up going to Assemblymember Daly's office after all. Right before we arrived, Phil turned to me and said, "Change of plans. We're meeting him on the assembly floor."

I stopped in my tracks.

The assembly floor is where real decisions are made in California. It's where history happens. It's not a place for spectators; it's where influence lives. And now I was being invited into it?

I kept walking, but my inner dialogue was on fire. *You are going to get exposed. You are not ready for this. You do not belong.* I kept walking anyway.

I was terrified. Terrified that someone would tap me on the shoulder the moment I stepped onto the floor and say, "Why don't you sit this one out?" I half expected it. In fact, I braced for it. I imagined it so vividly that I practiced my embarrassed smile in my head, thinking I would quietly bow out and pretend it didn't crush me.

But that moment never came.

Even though I was filled with doubt, I walked onto the assembly floor anyway.

No one tapped me out. No one questioned why I was there. No one even blinked. They just welcomed me in. They expected me to show up, listen, and engage . . . and so I did.

And while I stood there, in one of the most powerful rooms in the state, I had a moment of clarity. I remember looking around, feeling the weight of the moment, and then it hit me. I asked myself, *Why did someone I respect so much invite me here?*

Phil had seen something in me that I hadn't yet seen in myself. And I realized that maybe I didn't need to be 100 percent sure of myself in order to show up. Maybe I could borrow his belief until I found my own.

That moment planted a seed in me. It didn't bloom immediately. I didn't walk out of that room magically transformed, brimming with confidence. But something inside me shifted. I was terrified, and I did it anyway. I showed up when everything in me wanted to hide.

And that choice changed everything.

Proof You Are Becoming

If I had let doubt win, if I had let that voice in my head make the decision for me, I would have missed one of the most pivotal moments of my entire career. That single moment led to years of growth, more opportunities to lead, and a deepening commitment to advocacy. And eventually, it led me to something I never imagined:

Ten years later, I was honored to become the chair of the legislative committee for the California Association of REALTORS®, the largest trade association in California.

Let me say that again:

The woman who once sat in the back of the room, certain she didn't belong, now leads the committee that shapes real estate and housing policy for the entire state.

That didn't happen in spite of my doubt.

It happened because I didn't let doubt make the decision.

We have this deeply ingrained belief that confidence has to come first. That we're supposed to wait until we feel brave, polished, qualified, and absolutely certain before we step forward. We think we need to earn our way into courage, like there's a checklist we have to complete before we're allowed to take up space or try something new. We tell ourselves, *Once I feel ready, then I'll do it.*

But the truth is, confidence doesn't show up before the moment. It's not something that arrives at your doorstep with a ribbon and a guarantee.

Confidence isn't what gets you through the door.
Confidence is what you build once you've walked through it.

You earn confidence by moving forward while your hands are shaking, your heart is racing, and your brain is still trying to talk you out of it. You earn it by showing up anyway. And the more you show up in the face of fear, the more confident you become. Confidence is not the preapproval letter. It's the result of taking action.

We need to stop buying into the myth that successful people are fearless. They're not. Not even close. I've sat across from leaders, CEOs, founders, public figures, and top producers, and every single one of them has experienced deep, sometimes paralyzing, self-doubt. The difference is they didn't let it stop them. They didn't wait for the fear to disappear. They learned how to move with it.

They stopped seeing self-doubt as an enemy and started treating it as data. As information. As a message that something important was happening.

Because here's the thing: Self-doubt doesn't show up when you're playing small. It doesn't pipe up when you're doing something safe or familiar. It doesn't knock on the door when you're operating in your comfort zone.

Self-doubt only gets loud when you're standing at the edge of growth. It screams when you're about to do something that matters. It rises up when you're expanding, stretching, and evolving. That voice in your head, the one whispering, *You're not good enough. You're not ready.* That voice isn't proof that you're failing.

It's proof that you're becoming.

So instead of hearing that voice and shrinking back, I want you to hear it and lean in. Reframe it. Rename it. Realize it for what it is: *Self-doubt is the space where your confidence is born.*

It's a sign you're on the right path. That you're stepping into something that stretches you. That you are showing up in a way your past self might never have believed possible.

Self-Doubt's Big, Ugly Stepsister

But we can't have a conversation about self-doubt if we don't talk about its big, ugly stepsister, *imposter syndrome.*

I am the type of person who is tired of hearing about imposter syndrome being framed in a negative container, and I believe it's time we change that.

It's one of the most common and most misunderstood experiences high achievers face. It shows up when you're doing something new, when you're rising, when you're stepping into spaces your old identity never imagined.

Imposter syndrome is the lie that says, "You don't belong here." It's the fear that you're a fraud. That you've somehow tricked everyone into believing you're smarter, more capable, and more qualified than you actually are. It convinces you that success is a fluke and that at any moment someone will expose you.

We treat imposter syndrome like a diagnosis. Like it's a problem to fix or an insecurity to hide. But I want to offer a completely different lens:

Imposter syndrome is not a stop sign. It's a green light. It means you're growing. It means you've stepped into a space your previous self couldn't imagine. It means you're doing something that challenges who you used to be, and that's a good thing.

You don't feel like an imposter because you're a fraud. You feel like an imposter because you're expanding. You are literally in the middle of transformation. And of course that feels uncomfortable. Of course it brings up fear. Of course it makes you question everything.

That discomfort isn't disqualifying. It's evolution. So let's stop shaming ourselves for feeling imposter syndrome. Let's stop treating it as evidence that we don't belong.

In fact, I would argue the opposite: If you don't feel a little bit like an imposter every now and then, you might not be stretching enough.

Because the most successful, influential, and respected people I know still feel it. They still hear that voice. But the difference is they don't let it define them. They know it's part of the process.

They see it for what it is: forward motion. So the next time that voice tells you, *You're not ready*, I want you to ask yourself, *Or am I just growing?*

Quick Hits to Embrace Self-Doubt

Here's how to embrace self-doubt instead of letting it run the show:

1. **Name it.** Call it what it is. Say the words: "This is self-doubt." Speak it out loud or write it down. Once you name it, it loses the power to hijack your thoughts.
2. **Normalize it.** Everyone feels it. It's not a sign of weakness. It's a sign that you're stepping into something new. You're not broken. You're not behind. You're just human. And you're doing something brave.
3. **Reframe it.** When doubt shows up, reframe it as a sign that you're stretching. That you're on the right track. That something meaningful is on the other side. Instead of asking, "What's wrong with me?" ask, "What is this moment asking me to rise into?"
4. **Move through it.** You don't need to be 100 percent confident to take the next step. Take the step, and the confidence will come. Action builds evidence. Evidence builds belief. Belief builds confidence.

Self-doubt doesn't mean you're not enough. It means you care. It means you're trying. It means you're standing on the edge of transformation.

That moment—the one when your instinct is to back away, play small, and blend in—is not your cue to retreat. It's your invitation to rise.

As my friend and fellow keynote speaker Ryan Estis says, "Borrow my belief in you until yours catches up." So borrow belief if you need to. Borrow it from a mentor who sees something in you. From a friend who reminds you what you're capable of. From a coach, a teacher, or even a version of you from the past who did hard things and came out stronger on the other side.

Sometimes belief is contagious. Sometimes you just need to be reminded that you are, in fact, ready enough to begin. And if belief still feels out of reach, then do it scared. Do it anyway.

Take the shaky step. Make the uncomfortable call. Say yes before you feel ready. Because that one act of courage, the decision to show up despite the doubt, is the doorway to everything you've been dreaming of.

For me, that one act of courage led from the back of a crowded convention center to the floor of the California State Assembly. And years later, to a seat at the head of the legislative table. That brave, unsteady moment of saying yes opened the path to a future I couldn't have imagined if I'd let fear run the show.

I still feel self-doubt. It still knocks on the door. But I've learned to recognize it for what it is: not a disqualifier, not a warning, not a sign that I should sit it out.

It's a threshold.

It's a signal that something meaningful is waiting on the other side. And every single time I walk through it, I meet a stronger, more grounded, more confident version of myself.

Not because the fear disappeared.

But because I didn't.

And neither should you.

CHAPTER 5

Permission to Forget People Pleasing

Early in my real estate career, I thought that being liked was the key to being successful. If people liked me, they'd trust me. If they trusted me, they'd hire me. And if they hired me, they'd refer me. That was the formula I had written in my head, and for a while, I didn't question it. I became the person who said yes to everything, agreed with everyone, avoided conflict, and did whatever I could to be liked.

But underneath that approach was a quiet, constant exhaustion.

There's one memory I'll never forget: I was sitting at the dining room table of a 1950s tract home in Lakewood, my listing presentation spread out before me, trying to find the right words. The house had good bones—three bedrooms, one bath, a decent backyard—but it was showing its age. The kitchen cabinets were original, the bathroom still had the seafoam-green tile from the fifties, and the carpet had seen better decades. The location was solid but not premium—a quiet street in a good neighborhood, backing up to a busy road.

I'd run the comps three times. Similar homes sold between $750,000 and $775,000, and those were updated. This house, in its current condition, might fetch $800,000 on a good day.

But my client was convinced it was worth $900,000. He'd done his own "research" on Zillow and was certain his house was special. My stomach tightened. Every instinct, every year of experience, was telling me he was wrong. My jaw clenched. I started to sweat. I knew I should speak up, but I didn't. I just nodded and said, "Okay, let's get it listed."

The house sat on the market for four months.

Many times, a client would ask me to reduce my commission. I didn't pause. I didn't defend my value, my knowledge, or my experience. I just said yes. Over and over again.

Moments like these happened more than once. They happened for years. And each time, I walked away from the table feeling small. Feeling like I had given up something that mattered. Feeling like I had lost just a little more of my voice. I'd smile and say, "It's fine," but deep down, I knew it wasn't.

At the heart of it, I wasn't showing up as an expert. I was showing up as the performer. I was telling people what they wanted to hear, not what they needed to know. And that, my friend, is the opposite of leadership. That is the opposite of service.

People Pleasing Puts Your Power on Pause

Leadership isn't about keeping people comfortable; it's about helping them grow. It's about being willing to say the hard thing, the honest thing, even when it's not what they want to hear. When you're so focused on approval that you water down your message, you're not leading. You're placating. And while that might feel safer in the moment, it doesn't create trust. True service means honoring your role, your wisdom, and your responsibility to speak the truth with love. That's how you actually help people move forward.

We all have power inside us—our voice, our instincts, our truth.

But when we default to pleasing others at the expense of ourselves, we put that power on hold. We tuck it away. And in doing so, we give people a version of us that is polished, not powerful.

What most people get wrong about people pleasing is that they think it's kindness. They think it's being a team player. They think it's how you build relationships.

But people pleasing isn't kindness. It's self-protection. It's fear in disguise—fear of rejection, fear of conflict, fear of disappointing someone, and fear of being misunderstood.

And women—especially high-achieving women—are often the best at it. We want to be everything to everyone. We don't want to be seen as difficult. We don't want to lose relationships. So we say yes. We stay agreeable. We silence ourselves to avoid rocking the boat.

Although, let's be clear—men struggle with people pleasing too. Men, especially those in leadership positions, often experience pressure to be perceived as cooperative, agreeable, or nonconfrontational in order to maintain influence or avoid alienation. The truth is people pleasing isn't about gender; it's about survival. We all learn to modify our behavior to stay liked, accepted, or included. But that adaptation can cost us our authenticity if we're not careful. We want to be everything to everyone. We don't want to be seen as difficult. We don't want to lose relationships. So we say yes. We stay agreeable. We silence ourselves to avoid rocking the boat.

And it doesn't just show up in business; it shows up in friendships too. People pleasing in friendships looks like always being the one who adjusts, who cancels plans to accommodate others, and who listens for hours but doesn't feel safe sharing your own struggles. It's saying yes to things that drain you because you're afraid of being left out. It's being the dependable one, the supportive one, the strong one, even when you're falling apart. And over time, you start to wonder: *Do they even know the real me, or just the version I've been performing?*

You end up surrounded by people who like the image of you, not the truth of you. And that kind of friendship isn't a lifeline; it's a leash. You can't grow when you're constantly managing how you're perceived. You can't heal when you're pretending you're okay. And you can't build real connection if you're always the one doing the accommodating. Healthy friendships aren't built on obligation. They're built on mutual respect, truth, and the freedom to be fully seen.

People pleasing is draining. Emotionally, mentally, and physically. It doesn't just wear you down; it wears away at who you really are. You begin to second-guess yourself constantly, wondering if your words, actions, and decisions will upset someone. Your brain is always doing emotional calculus: *How do I make them happy? How do I avoid their disapproval?* And in doing so, you lose access to your own clarity. You can't think straight when you're constantly filtering your instincts through someone else's expectations.

It surrounds you with people who like the version of you that isn't even real, the agreeable version, the conflict-free version, the version who nods and smiles but stays silent when something doesn't feel right. And over time, that disconnection adds up. It keeps you stuck in relationships, jobs, and roles that aren't aligned with who you are but that you feel obligated to maintain just to keep the peace. You end up living a life that looks good on the outside but feels hollow on the inside. Because it's not actually yours.

Sound familiar? And the biggest cost? It keeps you from being fully trusted.

An Honest "No" Goes a Long Way

When you perform instead of lead, people eventually figure it out. They sense the disconnect. They start to question whether you believe what you're saying. And the trust that you were trying so hard to build? It breaks.

When I stopped people pleasing, everything changed.

In real estate, I started telling clients the truth, even when it was hard. I told them when their house was overpriced. I told them when their expectations were unrealistic. I stood firm on my commission because I finally understood that I was worth it.

And guess what? My business grew. People respected me more. They trusted me more. And they referred me more. Because when people know you'll tell them the truth, they want you in their corner.

The deeper I got into authentic service, the more trust I earned. Clients started calling me not just for transactions but for guidance. They'd reach out years in advance about market timing, send me listings for honest feedback, and insist I be the agent friends turned to for referrals, telling stories about how I'd protected them from costly mistakes.

In my speaking career, this shift was just as powerful. These days, if a speaking engagement isn't aligned—if I know deep down that I'm not the right fit for the audience or that I can't make the impact they deserve—I say no. That would have terrified me years ago. But now I know saying no isn't a rejection; it's respect. Respect for my time, for the audience, and for the person booking the event.

And when I do say no, I don't leave people hanging. I suggest another speaker who can serve them better. That's what real service looks like: not pretending I can do it all, but being honest about where I can do my best work.

Event planners trusted me with their most important events. When I said yes, they knew I was genuinely excited to serve their audience.

They sought my input on event design, knowing I'd help create the best possible experience rather than deliver a standard presentation.

Across both worlds, relationships became deeper, more collaborative, and more real. People weren't just hiring my services—they were inviting me into partnership with their goals and dreams. That kind of trust only comes when professional competence meets personal integrity.

Telling the truth doesn't make you unkind. It makes you trustworthy. Saying what needs to be said doesn't make you difficult. It makes you dependable.

There's a massive difference between being *nice* and being *real*. And the older I get, the more I choose real. These days, I measure success not by how many people like me but by how many people trust me. I stopped needing to be the favorite. I started needing to be the one who did the right thing.

And I'll tell you this: Laying your head on the pillow at night, knowing you acted with integrity, knowing you stood in your truth, knowing you didn't abandon yourself to make someone else comfortable—that kind of peace is priceless.

So how do you stop people pleasing but still show up with heart?

You stop saying yes when you mean no.

You start telling the truth with kindness.

You stop protecting people from discomfort.

You start trusting that honesty is love.

And you remind yourself: If your job is to lead, you cannot afford to perform.

But I need to warn you: When you first start breaking these people pleasing habits, it's going to feel wrong. Really wrong. Your body might actually react—your stomach might churn when you say no to a request, your heart might race when you set a boundary, and you might feel physically sick the first time you disappoint someone. This isn't a sign that you're doing something bad—it's a sign that you're doing something different.

For years, your nervous system has been wired to keep everyone else happy as a way to keep yourself safe. So when you start choosing yourself, even in small ways, your brain is going to sound alarm bells. You might feel selfish, mean, or ungrateful. You might worry that people will stop liking you or that you're being difficult. These feelings are normal, but they're not necessarily true.

The guilt you feel when you start setting boundaries isn't evidence that boundaries are wrong—it's evidence that you needed them a long time ago. The discomfort you experience when you stop over-functioning for others isn't a sign to go back to old patterns—it's growing pains from finally putting yourself in the equation.

Trust the process, even when it feels uncomfortable. The people who truly care about you will adjust to the new, healthier version of how you show up. And the ones who don't? That tells you something important about the relationship.

This isn't just true for real estate agents or keynote speakers. It's true for teachers, doctors, coaches, sales professionals, and anyone in a position of influence. If you're guiding others, whether you're leading a classroom, managing a team, consulting with clients, or simply showing up in your community, people need your clarity, not your compliance. Your honesty, not your sugarcoating. You cannot create transformation from a place of performance. You have to show up real. You have to show up rooted in what you know. Because leadership doesn't come from being agreeable. It comes from being aligned.

Small Reminders to Pause People Pleasing

Here's what I've learned along the way:

1. **Speak truth with empathy, candor, and care.**

You can tell someone something they don't want to hear with compassion. The delivery matters, but the truth still needs to be said. I always ask myself, *How would I want to hear this if I were them?* The next time a challenging conversation requires you to speak truthfully, take a beat to allow your emotions or nerves to settle before delivering your message. This ensures you're being thoughtful with your tone and language without infusing your own heightened emotions into the situation.

2. **Don't confuse peacekeeping with leadership.**

Avoiding conflict isn't the same as creating peace. Sometimes peace requires disruption. Sometimes it requires drawing a line. Sometimes it requires saying no. When you find yourself avoiding a difficult conversation to "keep the peace," ask yourself, *Am I actually solving this problem, or am I just postponing it?* True peace comes from addressing issues directly, not from pretending they don't exist.

3. **Your worth is not on the negotiation table.**

Your fees, your time, and your boundaries—those are not up for debate. When you know your value, you don't feel the need to justify it. Before entering any negotiation, write down your nonnegotiables. Know your minimum acceptable terms before the conversation starts so you're not making decisions from a place of desperation or people pleasing in the moment.

4. **Respect over approval.**

Not everyone will like you. And that's okay. You're not for everyone, and you're not supposed to be. Choose being respected over being liked. When you catch yourself changing your opinion or softening your stance just to be liked, pause and ask, *What would I say if I truly respected this person enough to tell them the truth?* Then say that instead.

5. **You can't serve and save at the same time.**

Your job isn't to rescue people from discomfort. It's to serve them with excellence and integrity. Saving them from hard truths doesn't help them. It only delays their growth. The next time you're tempted to soften feedback or avoid difficult conversations to protect someone's feelings, remember: You're not being kind by withholding information they need to succeed. True service sometimes requires letting people feel uncomfortable with reality.

I used to think that being nice would win me clients.

Now I know that being real is what earns their respect.

You are not here to be liked by everyone.

You are here to be fully you.

When you lead with that truth, you naturally attract the right people, the right friendships, and the right opportunities. People who see you, appreciate you, and want to walk alongside you.

Let go of the approval addiction. Let go of the fear of being misunderstood. Let go of the urge to say what they want to hear.

And instead, say what they need to hear—with love, with clarity, and with courage.

Because your power is in your voice. And you don't have to pause it to belong.

You don't need to abandon your truth to earn trust. You don't have to dilute your standards to keep a relationship.

Tell the truth. Be the expert. Say the thing.

And watch how everything changes.

Everything you've read so far is about coming home to yourself.

Because here's the truth: Before you can build deep, lasting, authentic relationships with others, you first have to build one with yourself. You are now ready to take this clarity, confidence, and courage you've cultivated and turn it outward—toward others, toward your teams, toward every relationship you touch. Let's go there next.

PART II

Your Relationship with Others

CHAPTER 6

The Foundation: Making People Feel Seen, Known, and Important

Six months ago, I was at an event for a speaking community I belonged to, and like most conference mornings, I needed my Starbucks fix. Hotel coffee just doesn't cut it for me, and thankfully there was one right next door. But instead of just grabbing coffee for myself, I did something different. I texted Jenny and Ivy, two of the staff in this community who had done so much for me, to ask their favorite Starbucks orders.

Jenny was the mama bear of the community—always smiling, always happy, always ready to help. She was a great connector, pivotal in introducing me to so many people, and an incredible dancer. Ivy was my coach and confidante, the speaker whisperer. She helped us see our blind spots, pulled out our best work, and was the best listener. Plus, she had thick, amazing red hair. (I may have been a little jealous.)

I got them their coffee that morning, and they were delighted. But here's what made the difference: I didn't just do something nice and forget about it. I put their coffee orders in my customer relationship management (CRM) app so I could remember them for later.

Six months later, we were at another event. Instead of asking if they wanted coffee (because I already knew), I just ordered it. I walked into the ballroom with their favorite drinks in hand—Jenny's go-to, a half-sweet vanilla latte, and Ivy's, a hot almond milk latte, extra shot, lightly sweetened with stevia.

The result was exponential. You can only imagine their reactions. Jenny had just walked across the room to tell Ivy something when I approached. Ivy squealed, and Jenny turned around, eyes wide with excitement. "I can't believe you remembered my exact order!" Ivy added, laughing. "Of course you did; this is what you do!" But more importantly, you can imagine how I felt knowing I had made them feel truly seen and remembered.

This wasn't just about coffee. It was about demonstrating that they mattered enough to me to pay attention to the details that brought them joy. At that moment, I wasn't just giving them caffeine. I was giving them the gift of being known.

The Difference Between Being Noticed and Being *Known*

There's a profound difference between someone noticing you and someone truly *knowing* you. When people notice you, they acknowledge your presence. When they actually know you, they acknowledge your humanity.

I experience this difference constantly. I'm always the one truly trying to know others (remembering people's fears, successes, challenges, and goals). I'm the one asking the follow-up questions, remembering the important details, and caring about what matters to them. But the reality is, very few people do this in return for me.

Most conversations I have are with people who only want to talk about themselves. They're not actually interested or curious about

But more importantly, they start to feel known. In a world where everyone is fighting for attention, the person who gives authentic attention and truly listens becomes irreplaceable.

The foundation of all meaningful relationships is simple: Make people feel like they matter. Because they do.

me. They might remember surface-level things about me—like how I don't eat gluten and I am deathly allergic to chocolate—but they don't remember the important things (the dreams I'm chasing, the challenges I'm facing, the victories I'm celebrating).

It's exhausting, honestly. I'll remember that someone's daughter just started college, their biggest client concern, or the vacation they've been planning for months. But when I share something equally meaningful about my life, I can see their attention drift. They nod politely, but I know they won't remember it next week, let alone next month.

The irony is that I've built my entire career on helping people feel known and valued, yet I often feel invisible in my own relationships. It's taught me firsthand the difference between being truly known and simply being acknowledged.

The neuroscience of feeling valued is simple enough for a twelve-year-old to understand: It's the feeling of truly knowing someone sees you, that you exist, and that you matter. It's the feeling of someone truly knowing you and not dismissing you or passing you by. When someone remembers what's important to you, your brain releases the same chemicals as when you receive a warm hug. You feel safe, valued, and connected.

When Relationships Turn Transactional

I recently agreed to hop on a call with a speaking colleague who needed help in the real estate industry. She wanted to know how to get more speaking opportunities in that space, and considering my background, she came to me. We had met before, and we had connected, but never on a deep level.

Our call ended up being all about what I could do for her. Not once did she say, "Now tell me about you," or "How can I help you?" It was entirely focused on her benefit. I found myself thinking afterward, *When was the last time someone asked me how I was doing and actually waited for the answer?*

This is what transactional relationships feel like. They're one-sided conversations where someone is taking without giving. These are the relationships where people only call when they need something. You can feel it in your gut when someone is talking at you rather than with you.

A transformational conversation would have looked different. She might have started by asking how I was doing, what was new in my world, or what challenges I was facing. She would have looked for ways to add value to my life before asking for value from it. She would have made the conversation about connection, not just collection.

The Relationship Trust Account

Here's a concept that will change how you think about every interaction: You have a relational trust account with every human you know. And every interaction you have with them is either a deposit or a withdrawal from that account.

When you make someone feel important through genuine recognition, you're making a deposit. Every time you remember something that matters to them, you're adding to their trust account. Every follow-up question, every thoughtful gesture, and every moment of authentic attention is a deposit.

But here's what most people get wrong: They try to make withdrawals before they've built up enough deposits. They ask for favors, seek introductions, or request help from people whose trust accounts are empty or overdrawn.

The coffee order example illustrates the compound effect of intentional deposits. The first coffee was a simple deposit. The second coffee—which occurred six months later when I remembered their orders without asking—was an even bigger deposit. It showed that they mattered enough to me for me to remember something seemingly small but personally significant.

The speaking colleague who called me for help was trying to make a major withdrawal from an account with very few deposits. She wanted my expertise, my connections, and my time, but she had never invested in building trust or making deposits in our relationship.

Now, before I sound too righteous, let me be honest: We all slip into withdrawal-heavy territory sometimes, often without realizing it. When we're hungry for growth or desperate for help, it's easy to fall into extraction mode. The key is noticing it and course-correcting before we damage relationships that matter.

That's why I make it a practice to lead with deposits whenever possible. Before I ask for anything, I pause and ask myself, *What have I contributed to this relationship lately? How can I add value first?*

Understanding Deposits vs. Withdrawals

There are several types of deposits we can make or receive in our relationships. Some of the most common include the following:

- Sending messages "just because" with no intention or ask
- Remembering important details about their life
- Following up on things they care about
- Offering help without being asked
- Celebrating their wins
- Supporting them through challenges
- Being present and engaged in conversations
- Sharing opportunities that might benefit them

The same goes for withdrawals, which oftentimes look like the following:

- Only calling when you need something
- Making every conversation about yourself
- Forgetting important details they've shared
- Being distracted during conversations
- Canceling plans consistently
- Taking credit for their ideas
- Asking for favors without having earned the right to ask for them

Building Permission to Ask

You have to build up that trust account before you ever have permission to ask for anything. Before you can say, "Friend, I need your help," you need to have earned the right to call them friend.

This doesn't mean you can never ask for help. It means you need to be strategic about when and how you ask. The deeper the trust account, the bigger the withdrawal you can make. But even then, successful withdrawals are followed by intentional deposits to rebuild the account balance.

The difference between knowing about someone versus knowing someone is like the difference between looking at a garden from the street and actually walking through it. When you know about someone, you see the surface, the well-maintained front yard, the obvious flowers, and the general layout. You can describe what you see from a distance.

When you know someone, you walk through their garden. You notice the hidden pathways, the struggling plants they're trying to nurture, and the special corner where they go to think. You see the weeds they're battling, the seasons they're in, and the dreams they're planting for next year.

Most people are content to admire gardens from the street. But relationships are built by those willing to walk through the gate, get their hands dirty, and truly explore the landscape of another person's life.

The Mathematics of Relationship Trust

The relationship trust account operates on simple mathematics, but most people never do the math. They make one deposit and expect to make three withdrawals. They remember your birthday once and think they can ask for business referrals for the next six months.

Here's the reality: Small deposits earn you the right to make small withdrawals. Big deposits earn you the right to make big withdrawals. But the account balance is always fluctuating based on your most recent interactions.

The most successful relationship builders I know don't wait until they need something to start investing in others. They're always focused on maintaining a positive balance in every trust account they hold. They make deposits consistently, not because they're planning ahead for withdrawals, but because they truly understand that strong relationships are built on a foundation of ongoing care, attention, and value.

They show up with kindness, follow through on promises, remember the little details, and offer support without expecting anything in return. Over time, these steady deposits create a deep well of trust that makes any future requests feel natural and welcomed, not forced or transactional.

Think of it like compound interest. The person who makes regular deposits into their trust accounts builds relationship wealth over time. But the person who only makes withdrawals finds themselves relationship poor, wondering why nobody returns their calls or responds to their requests for help.

When you consistently make deposits into someone's trust account, you create a compound effect that extends far beyond your direct interaction. People who feel valued by you become advocates for you. They trust you more deeply, engage with you more authentically, and open doors for you in ways that transactional relationships never could.

But more importantly, they start treating others the way you've treated them. Your intentional recognition creates a standard in their mind for how relationships should work. You become the example they point to when they talk about what genuine connection feels like.

The Connection Loop: Your System for Understanding Others

Now that you understand the relationship trust account, the question becomes this: How do you truly start to understand others? How do you move beyond surface-level conversations to really know what matters to people? This is where the connection loop comes in.

Here's the truth: Whoever understands the person the most wins. Every time.

In business, the salesperson who understands their client's real challenges, not just their stated needs, gets the deal. In leadership, the manager who understands what truly motivates each team member gets the best performance. In relationships, the person who understands what someone really cares about gets their trust, loyalty, and advocacy.

The connection loop is a four-step system that transforms casual interactions into deep understanding: listen, notice, document, and connect.

Connection Loop

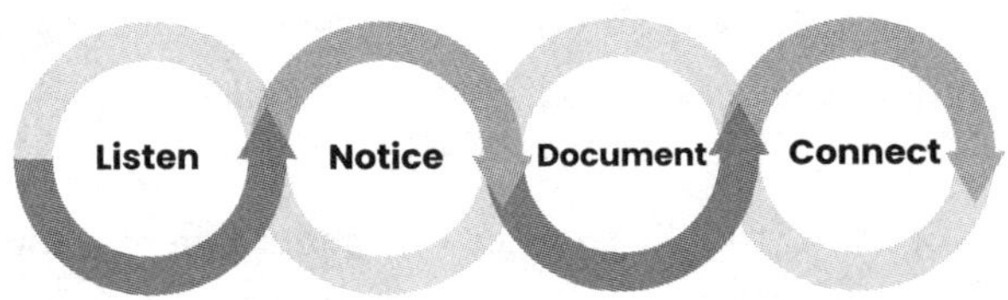

Listen (But Not to Respond)

Most people listen to respond, not to understand. They're already crafting their reply before the other person finishes speaking, missing the heart of what's actually being said. But true listening means being fully present. It means quieting your mind, silencing your phone, closing the tabs, and giving someone your full attention.

People are telling you everything you need to know—you just aren't listening.

People are always communicating what matters most—you just need to listen carefully enough to hear it.

Real listening isn't about interpreting or analyzing. It's about creating space. It's about making someone feel safe enough to share openly. When you truly listen, people feel it. They feel respected, valued, and heard.

Before you can notice or interpret anything else, first commit to simply listening.

Notice (Actually Notice Things)

Listening is just the first step—it's when you set the intention to let another person's ideas and energy into your mind. Noticing is the next step; it's when you actually absorb another person's message. You have to actively notice the details that most people miss:

- Notice their tone when they talk about different topics.
- Notice the words they use repeatedly.
- Notice the things someone almost said (you know when they stop halfway through a sentence).
- Notice their excitement (or lack thereof).
- Notice what they're drinking at the cocktail party or if they're not drinking at all.
- Notice if they seem tired, energized, distracted, or fully present.

The goal isn't to become a detective. It's to become genuinely curious about the person in front of you. Most people are so focused on themselves that simply paying attention makes you stand out.

Document (Write It Down)

Here's my superpower: I actually write it down. After an appointment, lunch, or networking event, I write down things I learned in my phone's notes app so I can then put it in my CRM or their contact record.

I document things like

- Personal details (spouse's name, kids' ages, upcoming vacations)
- Professional challenges (difficult projects, career goals, industry concerns)
- Preferences (communication style, meeting preferences)

- Emotional insights (what energizes them, what stresses them, what they're proud of)
- Favorite things (coffee order, restaurant, adult beverage choice, sports team)

Remember the coffee order story? I didn't just buy them coffee that first morning and move on. I documented their exact orders in my CRM. Six months later, when I showed up with their coffee without having to ask again, that's when the real connection happened.

Most people think they'll remember. They won't. The act of documenting shows that the conversation mattered enough to you to preserve it.

Connect (Apply What You've Learned)

This is the step everyone misses. You can't just notice all these things and document them. You have to actually do something with the information. You have to apply it to your connections.

If someone mentioned being nervous about a presentation, follow up afterward to ask how it went. If they're excited about their son's baseball season, ask about the games. If they told you they have an upcoming surgery, mark the night before or the morning of the surgery on your calendar so you can send them a thoughtful message.

Connection means acting on what you've learned. It's the difference between being observant and being relational.

When the Connection Loop Breaks Down

The loop can fail at any step; just because you start it doesn't mean you're honoring each step with intention.

- **Listen failures:** You're distracted, checking your phone, or thinking about your response instead of truly hearing them.
- **Notice failures:** You hear the words but miss the emotional subtext. You don't pick up on their energy, concerns, or excitement.
- **Document failures:** You have great conversations but don't capture the details. Three weeks later, you can't remember if their daughter is starting college or graduating.
- **Connect failures:** You have all the information but never act on it. You know their coffee order but never bring them coffee. You know they're stressed about a project but never follow up.

The most common failure point? **Connect**. People are great at gathering information but terrible at applying it.

Making the Loop Feel Natural

The connection loop isn't about being manipulative or calculated. It's about being intentional with your attention. If you struggle to remember or fully implement it, here are some strategies that make the loop feel more natural:

- **Set up simple systems:** Keep a note in your phone called "People I Care About," and jot down details right after conversations. The act of writing it down reinforces your memory, and having it accessible means you can reference it before your next interaction. And to really stay focused, take that information and put it into your CRM or their contact record in your phone.
- **Use calendar reminders:** When someone mentions an important event—like a job interview, a surgery, or a recital—immediately add a reminder for the day after to check in. For

example: "Ask Stephanie how Emma's piano recital went." This ensures your care translates into action.

- **Start small:** Don't try to implement the full loop with everyone at once. Pick two or three relationships that matter most and focus on them first. As the practice becomes natural, expand to others.

Remember, the loop works best when your attention is genuine: You listen because you're curious, notice because you're present, document because it matters, and connect because you care. The goal isn't to collect information about people. It's to create genuine moments of connection that make them feel truly seen and known.

The Daily Practice of Intentional Recognition

Making people feel seen isn't a grand gesture; it's a daily practice. It's remembering their favorite drink without being told. It's asking how their child's big game went last weekend. It's noticing when they're having a tough day and sending a quick message of support. It's celebrating their wins, big or small, and being there through the challenges.

The most successful people I know aren't necessarily the smartest or most talented. They're the ones who have mastered the art of making others feel truly seen, known, and important. They understand that relationships aren't built in big moments; they're built in small, consistent actions that demonstrate genuine care and attention.

When you consistently apply the connection loop, something powerful happens. People start to trust you more deeply. They share more openly. They think of you when opportunities arise. They become advocates for your success.

CHAPTER 7

Beyond Emotional Intelligence: The Power of Relational Intelligence

Emotional intelligence (a.k.a. EQ) has been praised as the secret to better relationships for years. In my own real estate career, it meant noticing when a client was stressed about a closing or when an agent was frustrated by a tough negotiation and responding in a way that calmed the situation. Those skills are useful, but I've also seen how they're not enough on their own to create real connection and trust.

One of the clearest examples of this came from a former colleague, Kylie. She could read a room like a book. She noticed stress, frustration, and excitement in an instant, and she responded with textbook empathy every time. By all accounts, she had mastered emotional intelligence.

But her team didn't feel seen. They respected her competence—but they didn't trust her with their vulnerabilities. Meetings ran smoothly, conflicts were de-escalated, yet people left feeling handled rather than heard.

Kylie was a manager in a busy real estate office, responsible for guiding a team of agents through high-stakes deals and demanding clients. On paper, she had every skill you'd hope for: the ability to spot tension, the know-how to respond calmly, and a solid grasp of people's emotions. But her team still felt disconnected, leaving her to wonder why her efforts weren't translating into deeper trust or engagement.

The problem? Kylie was so focused on managing emotions—both hers and others'—that she never went deeper. She treated people like emotional puzzles to solve rather than human beings to know and understand. She could read what people were feeling but couldn't translate that into genuine care or build the deeper trust that comes from truly seeing someone as a whole person.

We've mastered the art of recognizing when someone is stressed, frustrated, or excited, and we've learned to respond with appropriate empathy and support. And these skills are valuable. Emotional intelligence has helped countless people become better communicators, more effective leaders, and more empathetic colleagues. The ability to read a room, adapt your energy, and respond appropriately to others' emotional states is undeniably important in today's workplace and relationships.

But what, exactly, does emotional intelligence entail? To truly understand its power, we need to break it down into its core components. Traditional emotional intelligence focuses on three key areas.

Self-awareness: Understanding your own emotions and their impact on others. This means recognizing when you're stressed, frustrated, or excited, and understanding how those emotions affect your behavior and the people around you.

Self-management: Regulating your emotional responses appropriately. Instead of reacting impulsively when triggered, you pause, breathe, and choose a response that serves the situation better.

Social awareness: Reading others' emotions and understanding social dynamics. You can spot tension in someone's voice, notice when someone feels left out, or recognize when the energy in a room has shifted.

These are genuinely valuable skills. Someone with high emotional intelligence can walk into a tense meeting and immediately assess the emotional landscape. They can see that Tanya is stressed (tight shoulders, clipped responses), that Mark is frustrated (crossed arms, avoiding eye contact), and that Jennifer seems checked out (staring at her phone, minimal engagement). They can then adjust their approach accordingly, perhaps starting with acknowledgment of the tension, speaking in calmer tones, and creating space for people to express their concerns.

The Gap We're Missing

Here's what I've noticed: I've watched countless people with impressive EQ skills, people like Kylie who could read a room like a book and adjust their energy accordingly, still struggle to build the kind of lasting, meaningful relationships that create real influence and impact. They could identify emotions perfectly but somehow missed the human behind them.

EQ helps you navigate the emotional moment, but it doesn't teach you how to turn that moment into genuine connection and trust. It focuses on managing emotions in the present, but relationships are built over time through consistent care, genuine interest, and strategic investment in another person's success.

Emotional intelligence is like being a skilled weather forecaster. You can read the atmospheric conditions perfectly and predict what's coming, but you can't actually change the weather. You can manage the emotional climate of any interaction, but that doesn't necessarily mean you're building the foundation for lasting influence and trust.

Kylie had mastered the science of emotions but missed the art of connection.

Why This Matters More Than Ever

In our increasingly disconnected world, people are starving for genuine human connection. They can sense the difference between someone who's just managing emotions and someone who truly cares about them as a person. When you're managing emotions, there's often an underlying agenda; you're trying to keep your team moving forward, meet deadlines, accomplish an initiative, or maintain productivity. The person becomes a problem to solve rather than a human to understand.

But when you approach someone with genuine care and interest, your goal isn't to manage their emotions for a result. You're making space for the person and their experience without needing to fix them or move them along. You're present with what they're feeling, not trying to change it to serve your purposes. People notice this immediately; they can tell when they're being handled versus when they're truly seen.

Emotional intelligence focuses on the transaction: this moment, this interaction, this emotional state. But people don't just want their emotions to be managed. They want to be known, valued, and cared for as whole human beings. They want to work with people who remember what matters to them, who invest in their success, and who show up consistently over time.

The problem is that we've been so focused on understanding and managing emotions that we've forgotten emotions are just the surface layer of human connection. In a world where everyone is trained in emotional intelligence basics, something deeper becomes the differentiator.

As automation handles more routine interactions, the ability to build genuine human connections becomes a premium capability. Technical skills can be learned and replicated, but the ability to build trust, create influence, and inspire others through relationships remains uniquely human.

But here's what I've discovered: Emotional intelligence, while valuable, isn't enough anymore.

New Standard in Town: Relational Intelligence

This is where we need to go deeper than emotional intelligence. What if the goal wasn't just to manage emotions effectively but to build genuine trust and lasting connection? What if we focused not only on what people are feeling in the moment but also on who they are as whole human beings—complex, layered, and evolving?

Emotional intelligence teaches us to recognize and respond to feelings, but relational intelligence takes it a step further. It's about understanding the stories behind those feelings—the values, experiences, and motivations that shape a person's worldview. It's about moving from surface-level empathy to a deeper, more intentional way of relating.

My definition of relational intelligence is the skill of turning everyday interactions into lasting trust through genuine connection and strategic relationship building.

Emotional intelligence asks, "What is this person feeling right now?"

Relational intelligence asks, "Who is this person, what truly matters to them, and how can I show up in a way that creates a genuine connection that honors both their current emotional state and their deeper needs as a human being?"

It's a shift from managing emotions to nurturing souls. From reading signals to understanding stories. From reacting to feelings to investing in people.

This kind of connection doesn't happen by accident. It requires curiosity, vulnerability, and a commitment to being present—not just when it's easy, but especially when it's challenging. That's the power of relational intelligence: It transforms simple exchanges into meaningful relationships that stand the test of time.

As a leader, I quickly learned that relational intelligence wasn't optional; it was essential. Nowhere was that more evident than in my weekly real estate team meetings. Every Tuesday at 9:00 a.m., I'd watch as each person walked in, and I could see the usual emotional cues: Lauren's tight smile and the way she kept checking her phone, Jessica's slumped shoulders when she was discouraged about a deal falling apart, and Sarah's animated gestures when she was excited about a new listing.

Reading those emotions was just the beginning. The real insight came from understanding the relationship dynamics and whole-person context underneath.

Take Lauren's distraction. Someone with high emotional intelligence might recognize her tension and respond with empathy: "I can see you're feeling overwhelmed. How can we support you?" That's good, but it's not enough.

With *relational* intelligence, I knew Lauren's stress wasn't just about work. It was about her little ones at home. She'd mentioned in passing that her youngest had been having behavioral issues at daycare, and her five-year-old was struggling with separation anxiety. Her tight smile and phone-checking weren't just professional stress; it was a mother trying to manage crisis calls from daycare while maintaining her professional composure. She was evaluating whether this room felt safe enough for her to be honest about why she couldn't give 100 percent right now.

Then there was Jessica. While Sarah enthusiastically shared her three new listings, I watched Jessica's face. Someone with emotional intelligence might see her slumped shoulders and think, *She's discouraged about a deal*. But I knew Jessica hadn't closed anything in two months. Her mortgage was due, her kids needed preschool tuition, and Sarah's excitement about her success was probably feeling like salt in an open wound. Her slumped shoulders weren't just about one fallen deal. They were about questioning whether she could stay in this business and provide for her family.

Instead of just addressing surface emotions, we have to address the whole person.

Before we got too deep into our meeting details, I said, "Lauren, I know you mentioned your little ones have been going through some tough stuff lately. That has to be weighing on you. What would be most helpful right now?" Most of our team knew about how worried Lauren was about her kids, and bringing this up respectfully with the group let everyone see it was a safe space where we offer to help. After the meeting, I pulled Jessica aside. "Jessica, I can see you're carrying a lot right now. I want to show up for you. Can we grab coffee and talk about how to get you some momentum?" I asked softly.

The difference? Emotional intelligence saw the symptoms. Relational intelligence understood the whole person and the trust level that would allow them to be authentic about their real challenges.

When Relational Intelligence Changes Everything

I learned this lesson powerfully when a major business deal was falling apart. Three months of work, and we were down to the final hour with the buyer and seller at an impossible impasse over a five-thousand-dollar repair credit. Both sides had dug in their heels, and emotions were running high.

My husband, Harold, who's a master negotiator with decades of experience closing complex deals, tried every strategic approach in his arsenal. He presented comprehensive market data and offered creative compromise solutions. Harold has a gift for reading people and finding win-win scenarios that others miss. He's the guy everyone calls when deals seem impossible. But even with all his expertise, all the traditional tactics failed because this wasn't really about five thousand dollars. It was about something deeper.

That's when I remembered something crucial about the seller, Mrs. Chen. Six months earlier, during our initial listing appointment, she'd mentioned her late husband's workshop in the garage. She'd shown me his meticulously organized tools and shared how proud he'd been of maintaining their home perfectly.

I called her privately and said, "Mrs. Chen, I've been thinking about your husband's workshop. I remember you telling me how much pride he took in maintaining the house exactly the way he wanted it. I know the buyer asking for a credit to fix the issues in the workshop feels like a violation. This whole negotiation must feel like his standards are being questioned."

She was quiet for a moment, then said, "Yes. It feels like they're saying he didn't take care of our home."

"I understand. What if we framed this differently? What if we presented it as your final gift to the new family, helping them start fresh, the way your husband would have wanted?"

Twenty minutes later, she agreed to the credit. Not because of any logical argument or emotional management technique, but because someone had taken the time to understand the relationship between her emotions and her deepest values.

Harold had focused on managing the negotiation and the emotions in the room with surgical precision. I had focused on understanding the person and honoring what mattered most to her. The difference was everything.

This experience taught me that relational intelligence isn't just about managing emotions or reading the room. It's about connecting with the whole person and understanding their values, their history, and what truly matters to them beneath the surface. When you show up with that kind of empathy and intention, you create space for solutions that logic alone can't unlock. That's the power of relational intelligence: transforming transactions into trusted relationships.

Strategies for Building Your Relational Intelligence

So how do you develop this deeper level of connection? Relational intelligence isn't just an abstract concept. It's a learnable skill with specific practices you can implement immediately.

The Four Pillars of Relational Intelligence

1. **Relationship Awareness:** Go beyond reading emotions to understanding the history, trust level, and dynamics of your relationships. Before any important conversation, ask yourself, *What's the context of my relationship with this person? What do I know about what matters to them? What level of trust have we built?*
2. **Strategic Connection:** Intentionally build bridges between emotional moments and lasting trust. When someone shares something personal or vulnerable, don't just acknowledge it. Remember it and follow up later. If your friend mentioned getting some tests done last week, text her and ask how it went and if she needs anything.
3. **Systematic Investment:** Create deliberate practices that deepen relationships over time. This means keeping track of what matters to people, setting reminders to reconnect, and consistently showing up with value rather than just showing up when you need something. It's okay if you need a system or

reminder sometimes to jog your memory. It isn't impersonal; you're taking the time to ensure you remember what is important when it matters.

4. **Compound Thinking:** Recognize how today's relationship investments create tomorrow's opportunities. Every interaction is either building trust or spending it. Think long-term about the relationship, not just the immediate outcome. Whether the relationship is personal or professional, consider how you're hoping to help each other grow over the years. What do you want your relationship to look like decades from now, and how can you make sure you get there?

Three Practical Strategies to Start Today

Strategy #1: The Whole Person Check-In

Instead of asking, "How are you?" (which gets automatic responses), try, "How are things going with [specific thing they mentioned before]?" This shows you see them as a complete person, not just their professional role. For example, when someone mentioned their teenager was struggling with anxiety, following up weeks later with "How's Brooke doing with the anxiety issues?" demonstrates genuine care not only for your friend but for people they care about too.

Strategy #2: The Context Question

Before addressing someone's emotional state, consider the bigger picture. If someone seems frustrated, don't just manage the frustration. Ask yourself what you know about their recent challenges, their workload, and their personal situation. Then address the whole context: "I can see you're frustrated, and I'm thinking this is probably connected to all the changes happening with your team structure."

Strategy #3: The Value-First Follow-Up

When you reconnect with someone, lead with value for them rather than need from them. Send an article related to something they care about, make an introduction that could help them, or simply acknowledge something they've accomplished. This builds relational capital rather than spending it.

The Strategic Advantage of Deep Relational Skills

In a world where everyone is trained in emotional intelligence basics, relational intelligence becomes your differentiator. While others are reading emotions and responding appropriately, you're building the kind of trust that creates lasting influence.

People don't just want their emotions to be managed. They want to be known, valued, and cared for as whole human beings. They want to work with people who remember what matters to them, who invest in their success, and who show up consistently over time.

This is why relational intelligence isn't just a nice-to-have skill. It's becoming essential for anyone who wants to create real influence and impact. As automation handles more routine interactions, the ability to build genuine human connections becomes a premium capability.

The question isn't whether emotional intelligence matters. It does. The question is whether you're ready to go deeper, to move beyond managing emotions to building the kind of relationships that transform both your success and the lives of everyone around you.

Because in the end, people think it's about emotional intelligence, but it's actually about relational intelligence. It's not how well you can read emotions. It's how well you can turn those emotions into lasting trust and genuine connection.

That's where real influence begins.

CHAPTER 8

The VVR Factor: Visibility, Vulnerability, and Relatability in Action

Most people think building relationships is complicated. They overthink it, overanalyze it, and often overcomplicate it to the point where they never actually do it. But the truth is, meaningful connections come down to three fundamental factors that, when combined, create an almost magnetic pull between people.

I call it the VVR Factor:
Visibility, Vulnerability, and Relatability.

These aren't just nice-to-have relationship skills; they're the foundation of every meaningful connection you'll ever make. Whether you're trying to land a new client, build trust with your team, or deepen a friendship, the VVR Factor is your road map to authentic connection.

Visibility: The Law of Propinquity in Action

You can't build a relationship with someone you're never around. It sounds obvious, but it's the number one reason most people struggle with relationships; they're simply not visible or present enough to the people who matter.

The law of propinquity states that the greater the physical or psychological proximity between people, the greater the chance they will form a relationship. This isn't just about being in the same room; it's about being present, engaged, and consistently showing up in ways that matter.

There's a crucial difference between being strategically visible and being annoyingly self-promotional. Strategic visibility is about being genuinely present in spaces where you can add value. It's about showing up consistently, contributing meaningfully, and being someone people are glad to see.

Visibility isn't just about being seen—it's about being fully present when you are seen. There's a massive difference between showing up physically and showing up mentally, emotionally, and relationally.

You've experienced both sides of this. You've been in conversations with people who were physically there but clearly somewhere else—checking their phone, scanning the room for someone more important, or going through the motions of engagement while their mind was on their next meeting. Even though they were visible, they weren't present.

Then you've met people who made you feel like you were the only person in the room. They listened with their whole attention, asked follow-up questions that showed they were truly hearing you, and created a space where real connection could happen. Their presence was so complete that you left feeling energized and valued.

That's the kind of visibility that builds relationships. Not just being there, but being *all* there.

Think about that person in your industry who seems to know everyone.

It's not because they're working the room with a stack of business cards or forcing their pitch into every conversation. They're visible because they show up with genuine presence. They listen. They add value. They make people feel seen.

They're not "networking" in the performative sense—they're engaging. They're not chasing attention—they're earning trust. They're not everywhere at once—they're fully present wherever they are.

That's what true visibility looks like. It's not about being loud; it's about being real. And the authenticity behind that presence is what makes visibility powerful.

Here's where it gets interesting: Visibility doesn't look the same for everyone. And that's actually perfect, because authenticity is what makes visibility work in the first place.

Some people are natural extroverts who thrive in large groups and high-energy environments. They're the ones who can work a room of two hundred people and leave with fifty new connections. (Hi, that's me—I have an endless people tank and can be around humans for hours.) If that's you, fantastic; lean into it. But don't mistake volume for impact. Even as an extrovert, your goal should be meaningful connections, not just collecting business cards.

Others are more introverted or naturally reserved. They might prefer deeper, one-on-one conversations or smaller group settings. If this sounds like you, you might think you're at a disadvantage in building relationships. You're not. You're just playing a different game.

If you're naturally shy or introverted, the key isn't to transform yourself into some extroverted networking butterfly who works every room like a politician during election season. It's to find your people and your rooms. Trust me, they're out there; you just have to stop trying to fit into spaces that weren't meant for you.

Maybe it's a small mastermind group instead of a massive conference where you're lost in the crowd, surrounded by noise but craving real connection. Maybe it's a virtual community instead of an in-person networking event where you spend most of your time hiding in the bathroom. Maybe it's one-on-one coffee meetings instead of cocktail parties where you can't hear anything anyone is saying and end up nodding a lot and hoping you're responding appropriately.

The goal isn't to be visible everywhere; that's called being annoying, and nobody wants that. It's to be consistently visible in the right places and to the right people. It's about showing up intentionally where your presence matters most and your message resonates deeply. Being seen isn't about shouting louder or popping up constantly; it's about choosing moments strategically so you stay top of mind without overwhelming anyone. Remember, impact doesn't come from flooding someone's feed; it comes from making meaningful impressions at exactly the right time. Quality over quantity, always.

Vulnerability: The Strategic Art of Being Human

Let's start with what vulnerability actually is, because most people get this completely wrong.

Vulnerability isn't about emotional dumping or sharing your therapy session with strangers at Starbucks. It's not about being an open book to everyone you meet or turning every conversation into a confessional. Real vulnerability is strategic; it means being selectively open in ways that build genuine connection, guided by self-awareness and emotional intelligence to know when and how it's safe to share.

At its core, vulnerability is the willingness to show up authentically, even when you can't control the outcome. It's about being human enough to let certain people in at certain levels. It's about strategic openness that builds trust and connection without oversharing or making people uncomfortable.

Think of it like this: Vulnerability is about removing your armor, not your clothes. You're still protected, but you're allowing people to see the real you underneath the professional persona.

Recently, I experienced something that reminded me of both the power and the risk of vulnerability. Someone in my industry made an awful social media post about me, and let me tell you, if you were in our field—and if you knew me and this person—then you knew exactly who she was talking about. It was the kind of mean-girl BS that makes you wonder if we ever actually graduated high school.

My first instinct was to withdraw, and frankly, I did. I hid from social media for weeks, avoiding the platform that had become central to my business. When I finally came back, I made a choice that was genuinely me. I vulnerably shared my story. I talked about how it affected me, how it made me question everything, and how it reminded me that not every day is a unicorns-and-rainbows day, even when your Instagram feed suggests otherwise.

And because I'm an emotional creature who wears her heart on her sleeve (and sometimes on her face, in her voice, and in her entire body language), I got emotional. Really emotional. There were tears. Some people were uncomfortable with that level of rawness, and you know what? That's okay. Not everyone has the capacity to be vulnerable at the level I can or that I am comfortable with.

But here's the beautiful thing: The ones who leaned in, who said, "Thank you for being real," who appreciated seeing that successful people ugly-cry too—those relationships deepened in ways that a hundred perfectly curated posts never could have achieved. Turns out, people connect with authenticity, not perfection. Who knew?

If Vulnerability Feels Scary, Welcome to Being Human

Now, if you're reading this thinking, *There's no way I could share something that personal*, that's completely normal. Vulnerability feels risky because it *is* risky. You're essentially handing someone a piece of your heart and hoping they don't drop it.

But here's what I've learned: The people who matter won't drop it. And the people who do drop it? They just showed you who they are. That's valuable information too.

If vulnerability feels overwhelming, start small. Really small. You don't have to jump into the deep end of the emotional pool on day one. You can start in the shallow end and work your way up.

Here are a few baby steps to become more open:

- **Start with Safe People:** Share something slightly personal with someone you already trust. Test the waters.

  Example: When I was going through my hair loss journey, I finally told a close friend how scared and uncertain I felt. Her compassionate response reminded me that vulnerability often deepens trust rather than weakening it.

- **Share a Minor Struggle:** Talk about a small challenge you're facing, maybe a project that's harder than expected or a skill you're trying to learn.

  Example: I told my speaking coach I was struggling with transitions between main points. Admitting this challenge led to techniques that made me a much better speaker.

- **Admit When You Don't Know Something:** This is vulnerability in its most basic form. "I have no idea how to do this" is incredibly humanizing.

  Example: At one of my first speaking events, the AV team asked if I preferred a lavalier or Countryman mic. I admitted, "I honestly have no idea what you are talking about—can you explain to me the differences?" They appreciated my honesty, which made the setup process smoother.

- **Share a Genuine Compliment:** Sometimes being vulnerable means being the first to express appreciation or admiration.

  Example: "I really admire how you handled that difficult client situation. I would have been flustered, but you stayed calm and professional." It felt risky, but it opened a conversation about strategies we both use when feeling overwhelmed.

- **Ask for Help:** This requires vulnerability because you're admitting you can't do everything alone.

  Example: When my speaking calendar became overwhelming while I was managing my real estate business, I told Harold, "I can't keep up with everything. Can we figure out a way to redistribute responsibilities?" Admitting I wasn't superhuman led to systems that actually worked for both of us.

The key is to start where you are, not where you think you should be. Vulnerability is a muscle; the more you use it, the stronger it gets.

The Vulnerability Ladder

Not all vulnerability is created equal. No one would expect you to jump right into talking about your divorce or a recent diagnosis or a personal health goal with someone you just met or someone who you've only ever had superficial conversation with. There's a natural progression from the safest to the riskiest ways to open up.

Level 1: Professional Challenges

- Sharing a business mistake you learned from
- Admitting when you don't know something
- Asking for help or advice

Level 2: Personal Preferences

- Sharing what you're passionate about outside of work
- Talking about your family or hobbies
- Expressing your values and what matters to you

Level 3: Emotional Experiences

- Sharing a fear or insecurity
- Talking about a difficult time you've navigated
- Expressing genuine emotions about current situations

Level 4: Deep Personal Struggles

- Sharing ongoing challenges or hardships
- Discussing past traumas or significant life events
- Being completely authentic about who you are

The key is matching your level of vulnerability to the depth of the relationship and the appropriateness of the situation.

Relatability: The Art of Authentic Connection

Relatability is your secret weapon for turning strangers into allies and acquaintances into advocates. It's the ability to find genuine points of connection—the shared experiences, values, interests, or backgrounds that create natural bridges between people.

This isn't about pretending to be someone you're not or manufacturing fake commonalities. Real relatability comes from being genuinely curious about others and skilled at recognizing where your authentic experiences overlap with theirs. It's about finding the threads that connect us as humans and pulling on them gently to weave stronger relationships.

In my real estate career, I learned this lesson in the most practical way possible. When I would go on listing appointments, I was taught to walk around the house with a clipboard, writing down riveting details about the flooring ("hardwood, original from 1987"), windows ("double-pane, desperately needs cleaning"), room sizes ("optimistically described as 'cozy'"), and features ("that avocado-green bathroom from the seventies").

I realized I was missing the real opportunity and probably boring my clients to death.

Instead, during the entire "grand tour" with the seller, I started playing detective. But not for square footage, for connection points. I'd probe delicately for ways we could relate organically to each other. Did our kids both play baseball? Did we go to the same school? Did we share an interest in wine? Were there family photos that told a story I could relate to?

By the time we got back to the kitchen table, we weren't just agent and client sitting awkwardly across from each other. We were already connected. We had found common ground that made the business conversation feel like a continuation of a friendship rather than a sales pitch with a stranger who just critiqued your home décor.

Here's where some people get confused: They think being relatable means compromising their authenticity. That's backward thinking. True relatability actually requires authenticity; you can't connect genuinely with others if you're not being genuine yourself.

When I was connecting with those sellers, I wasn't manufacturing interests I didn't have. I was finding the parts of my genuine experience that overlapped with theirs. Maybe it was the shared stress of parenting young athletes and wondering if we should have taken out a second mortgage for all these tournaments. Maybe it was the pride in watching our kids grow and the slight panic about how fast it's happening. Maybe it was the financial investment we both made in our children's futures and the hope that they don't decide to quit right after we bought all the equipment.

The connections were real because they were based on truth, not performance. The goal isn't to be relatable to everyone—it's to be genuinely relatable to the right people.

When Your Nonverbals Sabotage Your VVR

Here's the thing about the VVR Factor: It only works when all parts of you are aligned. You can be visible, vulnerable, and relatable, but if your body language, tone, or facial expressions are sending a different message, you're essentially working against yourself.

I learned this lesson in the most humbling way possible, and it completely changed how I think about first impressions and nonverbal communication.

I learned this lesson the hard way when my friend Matt, one of my favorite humans on the planet, delivered some truth that hit like a friendly slap in the face. As we've gotten to know each other on a close level over the past few years, as true friends, not just colleagues who smile and nod at industry events, he's seen the real me. Recently, during one of our conversations, he dropped this bomb: "You know, you were so unapproachable when I first met you. I honestly thought you hated me."

Wait, what?

I have what people lovingly call RBF—resting b*tch face. Now, I'd always suspected this was a thing for me, but I had no idea how much my face had been sabotaging my relationship efforts throughout my life. Here I was, thinking I was being approachable, while my face was apparently serving up *Do NOT Disturb* vibes.

This was my wake-up call about how our body language and facial expressions can completely contradict our words and intentions. I might have been trying to be friendly and open, but my face was apparently broadcasting something completely different.

Now I'm intentional about my facial expressions, especially when meeting new people. I've learned to lead with a smile (a real one, not the creepy, forced kind), to soften my expression, and to be aware of the nonverbal messages I'm broadcasting. It's not about being fake—it's about making sure my outside matches my inside, and my inside is way friendlier than my face was advertising.

The VVR Factor in Action

When you combine all three factors—visibility, vulnerability, and relatability—something powerful happens. You become the kind of person others naturally want to be around. You create the conditions for authentic connection that goes beyond surface-level networking.

Each factor amplifies the others. Your visibility creates opportunities for vulnerability. Your vulnerability creates space for relatability. Your relatability makes people want to see more of you, increasing your visibility. It's a positive feedback loop that compounds over time.

The VVR Factor works in every context, but it looks different in each:

- **In Business:** You're visible at industry events, vulnerable about challenges and lessons learned, and relatable through shared business experiences.
- **In Leadership:** You're visible to your team, vulnerable about your own growth areas, and relatable through shared goals and values.
- **In Personal Relationships:** You're visible in your friends' lives, vulnerable about your authentic self, and relatable through shared interests and experiences.

Putting VVR into Practice

The VVR Factor isn't a theory; it's a practice. Here's how to implement it through the experience of someone intentionally building new professional relationships to open doors for future opportunities.

Increase Your Visibility: Imagine you're attending industry events and networking sessions with the goal of meeting potential collaborators.

- Identify two to three key environments where you want to build relationships.

  Example: You choose a professional association, a local industry meetup, and a quarterly leadership workshop.

- Show up in those environments consistently, not just when you need something.

  Example: You commit to attending at least three events per quarter, staying visible to the same group of people over time.

- Focus on adding value in every interaction.

  Example: You offer insights, share relevant resources, or connect people who might benefit from knowing each other.

- Be present and engaged, not just physically there.

  Example: Instead of scrolling on your phone, you actively listen, ask thoughtful questions, and remember details about the people you meet.

Practice Strategic Vulnerability: You start opening up selectively as you get to know new contacts.

- Start with level 1 vulnerability and work your way up as relationships deepen.

  Example: You share small professional challenges you're navigating, like learning a new software tool.

- Share lessons learned, not just successes.

  Example: You talk about a project that didn't go as planned and what you discovered from it.

- Be human about your struggles without making them the center of attention.

  Example: You briefly mention a tight deadline you managed, focusing on the strategy you used rather than dwelling on stress.

- Match your vulnerability to the context and relationship depth.

  Example: You save deeper, more personal disclosures for people you meet repeatedly and who have shown trustworthiness.

Find Genuine Relatability: You cultivate authentic connections that make people remember and trust you.

- Look for authentic points of connection, not surface-level similarities.

  Example: You discover a colleague also volunteered for the same nonprofit and bond over shared experiences.

- Share your genuine interests and experiences.

  Example: You mention a book or podcast that shaped your professional thinking.

- Ask questions that reveal common ground.

  Example: You ask about someone's approach to challenges in their role, leading to a conversation about shared problem-solving strategies.

- Connect through shared values and experiences, not just shared preferences.

  Example: You discover both of you value transparency and collaboration, creating a foundation for future opportunities.

The Long Game

The VVR Factor isn't a quick fix; it's a philosophy of relationship building that pays dividends over time. Visibility isn't about attention for attention's sake—it's about consistently showing up so people know you're invested in the relationship. Vulnerability isn't just sharing your story—it's about deepening trust and creating safety that encourages others to share theirs. Relatability isn't simply about being likable—it's about building bridges that allow genuine connections to form.

In a world that's increasingly digital, transactional, and disconnected, the ability to intentionally nurture visibility, vulnerability, and relatability becomes not just valuable—it becomes essential. The goal isn't temporary influence or short-lived attention; it's lasting relationships grounded in genuine human connection.

The question isn't whether the VVR Factor works. It's whether you're intentional enough to prioritize it, practice it, and build your relationships around it. Because at the end of the day, people don't connect with perfect—they connect with real. And real is exactly what the VVR Factor helps you become.

CHAPTER 9

Digital Relationships: From Screens to Real Connection

In a world where someone can have a million followers, the people who shape us most are often the ones with a few hundred or thousand. The friend who posts recipes you actually cook. The colleague who replies to your comment. The small but genuine connection that feels more powerful than a giant following.

And yet, despite these small moments of connection, loneliness is at epidemic levels. Even though we have more tools than ever to stay in touch, loneliness persists in America. Around 20 percent of US adults—about fifty-two million people—felt lonely most of the previous day in late 2024.* The surgeon general warns that social disconnection now raises mortality risk on par with smoking fifteen cigarettes a day and contributes to a 29 percent higher risk of heart disease, with equally steep increases for stroke and dementia.† How is this possible when

---

* Mary Page James and Dan Witters, "Daily Loneliness Afflicts One in Five in U.S.," Gallup, published October 14, 2024, https://news.gallup.com/poll/651881/daily-loneliness-afflicts-one-five.aspx.

† Juana Summers, Vincent Acovino, and Christopher Intagliata, "American Has a Loneliness Epidemic. Here Are 6 Steps to Address It," NPR, May 2, 2023, https://www.npr.org/2023/05/02/1173418268/loneliness-connection-mental-health-dementia-surgeon-general.

we have more ways to connect than ever before?

The answer lies in the difference between being connected and being in connection. We mistake followers for friends, likes for love, and engagement for intimacy. But here's what most people miss: Social media isn't the problem; the problem is how we use it.

Nowhere is this contradiction more apparent than in the influencer marketing era. We're surrounded by people with millions of followers who call themselves "influencers," yet influence has never felt hollower or more manufactured. The average person sees thousands of ads a day, many delivered by influencers who promote products they may have never used to audiences they've never met.

But here's what's fascinating: Even in this era of manufactured influence, authentic relationships still win. A Baylor University study analyzed over 1.8 million purchases and found that nano- and micro-influencers outperform macro-influencers on revenue per follower and return on investment (ROI), thanks to tighter, more personal audience bonds.*

The influencers who build lasting careers aren't the ones with the biggest follower counts—they're the ones who create genuine connections with their audiences. They respond to comments personally. They remember their community members' names and stories. They show up consistently, not just when they're launching something.

The most successful "influencers" I know don't think of themselves as influencers at all—they think of themselves as relationship builders who happen to have platforms. They understand that true influence isn't about reaching the most people; it's about genuinely impacting the right people.

---

* Maximilian Beichert, Andreas Bayerl, Jacob Goldenberg, and Andreas Lanz, "Follower Count vs. Engagement: Uncovering the Best Influencer Strategy," Baylor University: Hankamer School of Business, Keller Center for Research, September 1, 2025, https://kellercenter.hankamer.baylor.edu/news/story/2025/follower-count-vs-engagement-uncovering-best-influencer-strategy.

This is why micro-influencers (those with smaller, more engaged followings) often outperform mega-influencers in terms of actual business results. Their audiences trust them more because the relationship feels more real, more personal, and more authentic.

The influencer marketing era hasn't changed the fundamentals of human connection—it's actually highlighted how much we crave it. In a world of sponsored posts and affiliate links, genuine care stands out like never before.

Digital platforms aren't relationship substitutes; they're relationship accelerators. When used intentionally, they can create the foundation for the deepest, most meaningful connections of your life. I know this because it happened to me.

When Digital Becomes a Real Relationship

A lot of people I speak with and train tell me, "Barb, social media is a waste of time. You can't build real human relationships there." Well, I'm here to challenge that belief.

Ten years ago, I was scrolling through Snapchat when a profile randomly appeared in my feed. It was a woman named Chelsea Peitz, and she was different from everyone else. While others were posting selfies and food pics, Chelsea was dropping marketing tips for real estate agents. She'd share behind-the-scenes glimpses of her life—her dogs; her son, Mason; her husband, BP—but always with this authentic, helpful energy.

I found myself waiting for her posts. She felt like a friend I hadn't met yet, someone who was genuinely trying to help people while sharing her real life. There was something magnetic about her authenticity in a space filled with highlight reels and performances.

For months, I watched. I engaged. I developed what I now call a "fangirl crush"—not romantic, but that feeling when you genuinely admire someone and want to be their friend. My brain was treating Chelsea like a real friend, even though she had no idea I existed. I was investing emotionally in her success, feeling genuinely happy when good things happened to her, and developing a sense of connection that felt completely real. Because to my brain, it was real.

Finally, I got the courage to send her a DM. My hands were shaking—I felt like I was approaching someone I'd had a crush on for months, which, in a way, I was.

And she responded. Like a real human. Not with some automated response or cold reply, but with warmth and genuine interest. That single DM became the foundation of one of the most important relationships in my life.

But here's the thing: Our relationship didn't magically transform overnight. We stayed in the DM space for months. We weren't texting, calling, or video chatting. We were building trust and connection through short messages and continued social media interaction. I had to be strategic and intentional about deepening the relationship.

I remembered details from her posts and referenced them in our conversations. I shared my own vulnerabilities and challenges. I offered help and resources without expecting anything in return. I was applying the same relationship-building principles I'd use in person, just through a different medium.

Slowly, our digital relationship moved from Snapchat to Instagram, then to more personal DMs. We started sharing more about our real lives, our struggles, and our dreams. But we still weren't talking on the phone or video chatting. We were building something real through screens and pixels, one message at a time.

A year later, we were both attending Inman Connect, a real estate conference in San Francisco. I remember messaging her when I saw she was going to be there, asking if she wanted to meet up. Even though we'd been talking for months, I was nervous. *What if the connection doesn't translate to real life?* I'd thought.

I remember that first meeting like it was yesterday. I came down the elevator at the Hilton, looked across the lobby, and there she was—short platinum-blonde hair, looking at her phone, standing in line for coffee. It was like music went off in my head. And then I ran (yes, ran) across the lobby, screaming, "Hiiiiiiiii!"

I still remember the look on her face—half excited, half terrified at this fangirl who had just sprinted across a hotel lobby. But that moment sealed it. What had started as a digital connection became a real-life friendship.

Even then, I had to be intentional about maintaining and deepening the relationship. We exchanged phone numbers, but I didn't just assume we'd stay in touch. I followed up after the conference, referenced specific things we'd talked about, and made plans to connect again. I treated our digital relationship like the real relationship it had become.

Fast-forward ten years, and the relationship that started with a DM to a stranger on Snapchat has become one of the most important relationships in my life. But it didn't happen accidentally—it required years of intentional relationship building, trust development, and mutual investment.

Chelsea and I now do life together in every sense of the word. We talk every day across multiple platforms—sometimes simultaneously. We'll be texting while commenting on each other's Instagram stories while sending voice messages all at the same time.

We vacation together, bringing our families into each other's lives. We support each other through major life decisions, business challenges, and personal struggles. When one of us is going through something difficult, the other drops everything to be there. We celebrate each other's wins like they're our own.

She's been there through my biggest professional victories and my most challenging personal moments. I've watched her navigate career changes, family situations, and entrepreneurial ventures. We've built the kind of trust where we can tell each other anything—and we do.

What started as a digital acquaintance evolved into true friendship, then into something that feels more like family. Chelsea isn't just in my network—she's part of my inner circle, one of the people I turn to when I need honest advice, genuine support, or just someone who truly knows me.

And it all started with a DM to a stranger on Snapchat—and the intentional work over years to turn a digital connection into a real relationship. The initial spark happened online, but the depth came from consistent, strategic relationship building that honored both the digital foundation and the real-world connection we built on top of it.

The Parasocial Relationship Foundation

What I was experiencing with Chelsea in those early months was actually a well-documented psychological phenomenon: *a parasocial relationship*.

Parasocial relationships are one-sided emotional connections we form with people we don't actually know—celebrities, social media figures, and even fictional characters. Most people have experienced parasocial relationships, but few would readily admit to it. But here's what most people don't understand: These relationships aren't "fake" or "unhealthy"—they're using the same neural pathways as real relationships.

People regularly form one-sided, parasocial relationships with targets incapable of returning the sentiment. These relationships use the same psychological thought processes as real-life personal relationships. The human brain developed to be social, and when so much of our time is spent online or watching TV, we naturally apply our social cognition to digital interactions.

This is why my connection with Chelsea felt so real even before we ever spoke—because to my brain, it was real. I was using the same neural pathways I'd use to build any meaningful relationship, just through a different medium.

The Limitations of Digital Connection

But here's where the science gets really interesting—and where my story with Chelsea reveals something crucial about human connection. While digital platforms can create genuine relationships, recent neuroscience research shows they can't fully replicate what happens when we're physically present with another person.

Yale neuroscientist Joy Hirsch used sophisticated brain imaging to track real-time brain activity during conversations. Using a cutting-edge technology called *functional near-infrared spectroscopy* (fNIRS), her team was able to simultaneously monitor the brain activity of two people engaged in conversation—something that had never been possible with traditional brain imaging methods that could only study one person at a time.

In her groundbreaking 2023 study published in *Imaging Neuroscience*, Hirsch's team compared brain activity during face-to-face conversations versus Zoom conversations, keeping all other factors identical—the same people, same tasks, same duration. What she discovered was remarkable: Neural signaling during online exchanges was substantially suppressed compared to activity observed in those having face-to-face conversations.* In other words, our brains literally work differently—and work harder—when we're connecting through screens.

Montreal researchers found that when conversations take place through a screen versus face-to-face, "our brains work a lot harder to make a connection with others." Using brain monitoring technology, they discovered nine key "cross-brain links" between people in the same room, but only one link during video conversations.†

This explains so much about my relationship with Chelsea. Yes, we built something real through DMs and social media—my brain was genuinely connecting with her using the same neural pathways as any friendship. But that magical moment when I ran across the hotel lobby? That's when our relationship shifted into an entirely different gear. I was seeing her in person for the first time, and her energy and personality were palpable—our friendship and connection became so much stronger.

The digital foundation was essential, but the face-to-face connection was transformational.

This doesn't mean digital relationships are inferior—it means they're the *beginning*, not the destination. Understanding this limitation actually makes you more strategic: When you know that screens suppress neural connections, you become more intentional about moving important relationships into real life.

The most powerful digital relationships are the ones that eventually transcend the digital space. They start with a DM, develop through

---

* Bill Hathaway, "Zooming in on Our Brains on Zoom," *YaleNews*, October 25, 2023, https://news.yale.edu/2023/10/25/zooming-our-brains-zoom; Nan Zhao, Xian Zhang, J. Adam Noah, Mark Tiede, and Joy Hirsch, "Separable Processes for Live 'In-Person' and Live 'Zoom-like' Faces," *Imaging Neuroscience* 1, (2023): https://direct.mit.edu/imag/article/doi/10.1162/imag_a_00027/117875/Separable-processes-for-live-in-person-and-live.

† Staff report, "Neuroscience Explains Why Video Calls Are So Exhausting," Psychiatrist.com, January 18, 2023, https://www.psychiatrist.com/news/neuroscience-explains-why-video-calls-are-so-exhausting/.

consistent online interaction, and then flourish when they move into the physical world, where our brains can fully connect.

The Platform-Specific Relationship Strategy

Not all social media platforms are created equal for relationship building. Each has its own culture, rhythm, and opportunity for connection. Here's how to approach each strategically, in order of my personal favorites for building genuine relationships.

Instagram: Visual Storytelling for Connection

Instagram is where authenticity meets aspiration. It's perfect for showing the human side of your professional life and finding common ground with others. This is my absolute favorite platform for relationship building because it allows for both polished content and authentic behind-the-scenes moments.

Here is my Instagram connection strategy:

- **Stories Over Posts:** Use Stories to share behind-the-scenes moments, quick tips, and real-time updates. This creates intimacy and invitation.
- **Meaningful Comments:** Instead of emoji reactions, leave thoughtful comments that start conversations. Ask questions, share experiences, and offer encouragement.
- **The DM Bridge:** Use direct messages to move conversations deeper. Reference something specific from their content to show you're paying attention.

LinkedIn: The Professional Relationship Accelerator

LinkedIn isn't just for job hunting; it's for building your career through relationships. But most people approach it completely wrong. They send generic connection requests, post dry company updates, and share nothing personal. They make it all about business and strategy and then wonder why nothing meaningful ever happens.

Here is my LinkedIn connection strategy:

- **Connect with Context:** Never send a blank connection request. Reference where you met, what you admired about their work, or a specific reason you want to connect.
- **Value-First Engagement:** Comment thoughtfully on posts. Share insights, ask questions, and offer help. Don't just hit Like and move on.
- **The Follow-Up Formula:** When someone accepts your connection, send a personal message within twenty-four hours. Not a sales pitch—a genuine thank-you and conversation starter.

Facebook: Community Building and Deeper Engagement

Facebook excels at community building and maintaining ongoing relationships. It's where casual connections can become meaningful ones, especially through groups and shared interests.

Here is my Facebook connection strategy:

- **Group Participation:** Join groups relevant to your interests and industry. Contribute valuable content and build relationships with other active members.

- **Event Engagement:** Attend virtual and in-person events. Follow up with new connections on Facebook to continue conversations.
- **Personal Sharing:** Share personal updates, celebrations, and challenges. This creates opportunities for others to connect with you on a human level.

What NOT to Do: The Digital Relationship Killers

Before we move into advanced strategies, let's address the biggest mistakes people make that destroy digital relationships before they even begin. These approaches are not just ineffective—they're relationship repellant.

A good example is LinkedIn, where digital relationship building goes to die, and it's usually because people treat it like a vending machine instead of a networking venue. Here are the cardinal sins that will get you blocked, ignored, or worse—remembered for all the wrong reasons.

You know exactly what I am talking about. You know this person. They send a connection request, you accept thinking you might want to network, and within thirty seconds you get a message like, "Hi! Thanks for connecting! I help [generic business category] increase their revenue by three hundred percent through our proven system. I'd love to hop on a quick fifteen-minute call to see how we can help your business grow! Here's my calendar link!"

This is the digital equivalent of walking up to someone at a party, shaking their hand, and immediately asking them to buy something. It's transactional, impersonal, and completely relationship killing.

Even worse are the obvious automated responses. You can spot them immediately:

- Generic language that could apply to anyone
- Immediate responses (like, suspiciously immediate)
- No reference to anything specific about you or your business
- Calendar links in the first message
- Copy-paste feel with obvious template language

This person's entire LinkedIn strategy revolves around getting you on a call. They'll say things like:

- "I'd love to learn more about your business!" (Translation: "I want to pitch you!")
- "Let's hop on a quick call to see how we can help each other!" (Translation: "Let me sell you something.")
- "I'm always looking to connect with like-minded professionals!" (Translation: "You seem like a good prospect.")

Then there's the spray-and-pray approach. These are the people who send identical messages to hundreds of connections, hoping someone will bite. The dead giveaways:

- Messages that could apply to literally anyone
- Generic compliments about your "impressive profile"
- No mention of anything specific about your actual work or content
- The same message you've seen them send to others in your network

When you lead with a transactional approach, you're essentially saying, "I don't see you as a person worth knowing—I see you as a potential customer." This immediately puts people on the defensive and destroys any possibility of real connection.

Here's what happens in the recipient's brain:

1. **Immediate Distrust:** "This person doesn't actually care about me."
2. **Defensive Reaction:** "I need to protect myself from being sold to."
3. **Relationship Prevention:** "I will never engage with this person meaningfully."
4. **Network Contamination:** "I'll warn others about this person's approach."

The irony is that these tactics don't even work for business development. People buy from people they trust, and trust can't be built through automated pitch sequences and calendar links.

The Relationship-First Approach

Chelsea, who happens to be a social media expert, once asked me a question that completely changed how I show up online: "What would you do in person?" If you ran into someone at the grocery store who mentioned they were going through a tough time, you wouldn't hand them your business card and start talking about your services. You'd ask how they're doing, listen, and offer support if you could.

The same principle applies online. When someone shares something meaningful—a professional milestone, a personal struggle, a moment of excitement or vulnerability—they're having a conversation in a public space. How you respond determines whether you're someone who truly sees them or someone who's just waiting for their turn to talk.

Instead of leading with what you want, lead with what you can give:

- Reference something specific from their content.

- Share a genuine insight or observation.
- Ask a thoughtful question about their work.
- Offer a resource or connection that might help them.
- Simply acknowledge their expertise or contribution.

People who build lasting relationships on social media respond to the human behind the post, not the potential opportunity. They celebrate wins without asking for introductions, offer support without expecting anything in return, and engage because they're genuinely interested.

When you consistently show up as someone who cares beyond what others can do for you, people begin to trust you. They think of you when opportunities arise and refer others because they know you'll treat them well.

Remember: The goal of the first message isn't to sell something or book a call. The goal is to start a conversation and show that you're a real human who pays attention.

The Digital-to-Physical Bridge

Digital connections are valuable, but the real magic, the kind that builds lifelong relationships, happens offline. I've seen so many people stop short right here: They nurture great conversations online, exchange comments and likes, but they never take it further. And that's a missed opportunity.

As we've both experienced and seen proven in the research, relationships deepen when you move from screens to face-to-face conversations. So once you've established some genuine digital rapport, take a moment to thoughtfully create an opportunity to meet in person.

Here's how it usually looks: You genuinely enjoy someone's content or conversation, and you mention something specific that resonated with you. Maybe you notice they're attending a conference nearby or you're traveling to their area, and you casually suggest grabbing coffee or meeting up. It doesn't have to be complicated; a simple, low-pressure invitation often leads to the most meaningful conversations.

Once they say yes, follow through in a way that shows your commitment. Send a calendar invite promptly. Text or email the day before to confirm and share your cell number for easy communication. Show up early and fully present with your phone tucked away. And afterward, reach out again with a simple thank-you and a natural next step. Relationships aren't built in one conversation; they're built through ongoing, intentional connection.

I've learned over the years that relying solely on spontaneous meetings rarely leads to consistent relationship building. Now I intentionally create opportunities to connect in person. If there's an industry event, I'll do some homework: I'll see who's attending, connect online beforehand, and set up specific times to meet face-to-face. Afterward, I'll follow up personally, referencing our conversation, and let them know I genuinely valued the interaction.

Or better yet, I'll organize my own gatherings, small dinners, casual coffee meetups, or even a happy hour. I invite digital connections to join, creating an intimate environment that naturally fosters deeper conversations. This approach not only builds stronger relationships, but it also shows I'm committed enough to create a space specifically designed for connection.

Building the bridge from digital to physical takes effort and intentionality, but it's always worth it. Because when you move past screens and into real life, that's when connections become friendships, partnerships, and relationships that truly matter.

Content as Relationship Currency

Your content isn't just about building an audience—it's about building relationships. Every post, comment, and share is an opportunity to connect with someone.

In chapter 8, we discussed the VVR Factor—visibility, vulnerability, and relatability. We're going to take it a step further and discuss the VVR Factor at play as a content strategy in the digital world. Here is how you can apply the VVR Factor to your digital content:

Visibility: Be consistently present and valuable.

- Share insights regularly, not just when you need something.
- Comment meaningfully on others' content.
- Show up authentically in your own content.

Vulnerability: Share the real story, not just the highlight reel.

- Talk about challenges and failures, not just successes.
- Ask for help and advice from your network.
- Share what you're learning, not just what you know.

Relatability: Find common ground through shared experiences.

- Reference popular culture, current events, or universal experiences.
- Share personal stories that others can connect with.
- Ask questions that invite others to share their own experiences.

Because in the end, it's not about how many people see your content. It's about what that content leads to. Stop measuring followers and start measuring relationships. It doesn't matter how many people follow you; it matters how deeply you're connecting with them. Instead of chasing superficial numbers, pay attention to what actually moves the needle: how many meaningful conversations you're starting, how often your digital connections become real-world meetings, the referrals and opportunities that come from genuine relationships, and the depth of engagement you're creating.

The Intentionality Factor

The difference between digital networking and digital relationship building is intention. When Chelsea showed up in my feed, I could have just watched passively. Instead, I chose to engage. I chose to be vulnerable with that first DM. I chose to maintain the connection across platforms and time. Most importantly, I chose to be patient and strategic about moving from digital connection to real relationship.

That choice—to be intentional rather than accidental or random—transformed a random social media encounter into one of the most important relationships in my life. But it didn't happen overnight, and it didn't happen by accident. It required the same intentional effort as any meaningful relationship, just applied through digital channels.

The Strategic Patience Principle

One of the biggest mistakes people make with digital relationships is trying to rush them. They want to move from connection request to best-friend status overnight. Real relationships don't work that way, and neither do digital ones.

With Chelsea, I spent months building trust through consistent, valuable interactions. I didn't ask for anything. I didn't try to move the relationship too quickly. I let it develop naturally while being intentional about adding value and showing genuine interest in her life and work.

This strategic patience is crucial in digital relationship building. Trust develops over time through consistent actions, not grand gestures. The compound effect of small, regular interactions creates stronger foundations than sporadic, intense exchanges.

Digital relationships require vulnerability to move from surface-level to meaningful. But this vulnerability must be strategic—sharing at the right time, in the right way, and in the right amount.

When I first messaged Chelsea, I was vulnerable about being a fan of her work. I shared specific things I'd learned from her content and how they'd helped me. This wasn't just flattery—it was authentic vulnerability that showed I'd been paying attention and genuinely valued what she was sharing.

As our relationship developed, I continued to share challenges I was facing, ask for advice, and offer support when she shared her own struggles. This gradual increase in vulnerability created the trust and intimacy that transformed our digital connection into a real friendship.

We're living through a digital relationship revolution. The tools for connection have never been more powerful, but most people are using them wrong.

They're collecting contacts instead of cultivating relationships. They're building audiences instead of building community.

But when you approach digital platforms with the same intentionality you'd bring to any meaningful relationship, magic happens. Strangers become friends. Connections become collaborators. Followers become family.

The question isn't whether digital relationships are "real"—Chelsea and I prove they are. The question is whether you'll be intentional enough to build them.

Your Digital Relationship Action Plan

Whether you have an established social media presence, a few forgotten accounts, or you're just now considering joining any of the platforms, following this digital relationship action plan will provide you with thoughtful, strategic direction that will prevent you from aimlessly scrolling, commenting, and liking without any intentionality. Take some time to walk yourself through the steps below:

1. **Audit Your Current Approach:** How are you currently using social media? For consumption or connection?
2. **Choose Your Platforms:** Pick one to two platforms where your ideal connections spend time. Go deep, not wide.
3. **Develop Your VVR Strategy:** Plan how you'll be visible, vulnerable, and relatable on each platform.
4. **Create Connection Systems:** Set up processes for moving digital connections to real-world relationships.
5. **Measure What Matters:** Track relationship depth, not vanity metrics.
6. **Be Patient:** Real relationships take time to develop, whether they start online or offline.

Remember: Every meaningful relationship started with a first interaction. In our digital age, that first interaction might be a DM, a comment, or a connection request. The medium has changed, but the fundamentals remain the same: Be genuine, be helpful, and be human.

Your next best friend, business partner, or life-changing connection might be one DM away. The question is, are you brave enough to send it?

In a world where everyone is trying to get noticed, the real opportunity is in making others feel seen. Digital platforms don't change this truth—they amplify it.

CHAPTER 10

The Relationship Operating System: When Good Intentions Meet Strategic Action

Let's get something straight: Intention without action is just wishful thinking.

Maybe you meet someone at a networking event and have an incredible conversation—you swap stories, feel a real connection, and leave excited to follow up. Then you get home, dive back into life, and that message never gets sent.

Or maybe you think of a friend or mentor who's been on your mind, someone who always lifted you up—but you tell yourself you'll reach out when things "slow down." Weeks pass, and so does the moment.

It's not because you don't care. It's because caring isn't enough.

The difference between people who build influential networks and people who wonder why their network doesn't respond isn't the depth of their intention—it's the strength of their systems.

Here's what nobody wants to hear: If you're serious about relationships being your competitive advantage, you need to get systematic about them. This isn't transactional; it's intentional.

There's a massive difference.

Transactional systems ask, "What can I get?"

Intentional systems ask, "What can I give?"

Transactional approaches follow scripts. Intentional approaches create authentic moments. Transactional systems treat people like ATMs. Intentional systems treat relationships like investments. The best relationship builders aren't always the most naturally gifted at connection; they're the most intentional about creating it.

Every Opportunity Is a Relationship

Think about the biggest opportunities in your life. The job that changed your trajectory. The introduction that led to your biggest client. The conversation that sparked your best idea. The connection that opened the door you'd been trying to unlock.

Behind every single one was a relationship.

Not a transaction. Not a cold email. Not a perfect LinkedIn message. It started with a relationship with a human being who knew you, trusted you, and chose to help you.

Now think about all the relationships you've let drift away. The people you meant to stay in touch with. The connections you made but never nurtured. The introductions you received but didn't follow up on.

Every one of those could have been an opportunity you missed.

Here's what most people don't want to face:

**Relationships aren't just nice to have—
they're your competitive advantage.**

And competitive advantages require strategy, not just good intentions.

You know the feeling. You think about someone and make a mental note to reach out. Days pass. Weeks pass. Suddenly it feels awkward because it's been too long. So you put it off even longer. Before you know it, you're that person who shows up in someone's life only when you need something—or not at all.

The relationships that could have been your greatest advocates become strangers. The connections that could have opened doors drift away. The people who could have changed your trajectory forget you exist.

Not because you don't care. Because caring without action is just wishful thinking.

The Speed of Intentional Relationships

Here's the problem with good intentions: They live entirely in your head. They sound like "I should reach out," or "I meant to follow up," or "I've been thinking about calling them." But here's the truth: No one feels your intention until it becomes *action*.

This is what "just intention" looks like:

- **Good ideas without follow-through**—thinking about people but never actually connecting.
- **Hustle without depth**—chasing numbers and followers instead of investing in people.
- **Self-centered energy**—meaning well but never moving the needle for anyone else because the intention stays trapped inside your head.

In other words, intention is invisible until it's expressed. Trust isn't built by what you meant to do—it's built by what you actually did.

When you move from intention to intentional relationships:

- You don't just think about people—you reach out.
- You don't just want trust—you systematically invest in it.
- You don't just hope for referrals—you earn them through consistent care.
- You don't just plan for growth—you build the relationships that create it.

This is why successful relationship builders don't move at the speed of intention—they move at the speed of intentional relationships. Because while intention feels good, intentional action creates results.

To move at the speed of intentional relationships, you need a simple, repeatable system. One that ensures your best intentions turn into meaningful action.

The Relationship Operating System: Five Components That Change Everything

Here's what I've learned after years of studying how the most connected people actually operate: They don't just have better intentions—they have better systems.

The Relationship Operating System has five core components that work together to turn your network into your net worth.

1. **Ranking:** Know exactly what level each relationship is at so you can invest your time and energy strategically, not randomly.
2. **Mindset:** Develop daily habits that transform good intentions into consistent relationship-building action.

3. **Frequency:** Use strategic timing based on relationship levels to prevent drift and deepen connections.
4. **Handwritten Notes:** Harness the power of personalized, tangible communication to make memorable, lasting impressions.
5. **Moment-Based Touches:** Show up authentically during life's meaningful moments—the big and the small—to create connection magic.

These aren't separate tactics; they're interconnected parts of a system that ensure your most important relationships get the attention they deserve while preventing you from burning out trying to be everything to everyone.

Let's break down each piece so you can start building relationships that actually compound your influence.

Component #1: Relationship Ranking System—Know Your Relationship Levels

Before you can be strategic about relationships, you have to get honest about something most people won't admit: You can't maintain the same level of closeness and investment with everyone you know.

On the surface, this might seem obvious, but in practice, many people act like it isn't. They try to be equally close to everyone, equally available to all, and equally invested in every connection. They spread themselves too thin, hoping to keep all relationships afloat with the same effort. It's exhausting, unsustainable, and ultimately ineffective.

The truth is no one has unlimited time, energy, or emotional bandwidth. Even the most outgoing, connected people have boundaries—whether they name them or not. The key difference is whether you're intentional about those boundaries or if you're just hoping for the best and reacting as things come.

In reality, you already have different levels of relationships in your life—across friendships, business, work, and family. Some people are your closest confidants, others are casual acquaintances, and everything in between. The difference between thriving and surviving relationally comes down to recognizing those levels and showing up accordingly.

The first step to building a Relationship Operating System is this: Get crystal clear about exactly what level each relationship is at. This clarity allows you to invest your time, energy, and attention appropriately—nurturing your inner circle deeply, maintaining regular contact with those who matter, and letting others naturally stay more distant without guilt or overwhelm.

If you're just beginning, don't overcomplicate it. A simple Google Sheet, Excel document, or even a dedicated notebook can help you track names, categories, and next steps. What matters most is building the habit of intentional tracking.

As your network grows and your system becomes more robust, you may want to transition to a dedicated customer relationship management (CRM) platform. Tools like Airtable, HubSpot, or Notion can help automate reminders, organize contact details, and make it easier to follow up consistently. The most successful relationship builders don't rely on memory; they rely on systems that keep their best intentions from slipping through the cracks.

When you get honest about this, you stop chasing impossible standards and start focusing on what truly moves your relationships forward.

The Five Levels (and Why They Matter)

★★★★★ ADVOCATES: YOUR INNER CIRCLE

These are the absolute closest people to you. Your best friends. Your best clients. The people on your own personal board of directors. Some family members. (Hey, not all family members deserve this level.) These are the relationships that change your life because they're not just rooting for you; they're actively invested in your success.

Business Example: Your best client, who not only gives you their business but also refers you to their network and values your advice on important choices.

Friend Example: Your closest friend, whom you call when you need to make a big life decision and who genuinely cares about your happiness and success—and who checks in on you when you're quiet.

★★★★☆ CHAMPIONS: CLOSE, BUT NOT AS DEEP

Champions are the people who are close to you, just not as deep as your advocates. The difference between five-star and four-star relationships is often subtle, but you know it when you feel it. Sometimes it's just not as frequent. Not as intentional. But the care and support is genuine.

Business Example: A valued client you enjoy great conversations with and who refers you to others but with whom you don't yet have the deeper, strategic relationship you have with your best clients.

Friend Example: A close friend whom you love spending time with and who always supports your goals, but who isn't your first call when something major happens in your life.

★★★☆☆ CONNECTIONS: YOU KNOW THEM; THEY KNOW YOU

You know them; they know you. You'd recognize them in the grocery store and have a real conversation. There's mutual recognition and respect, but the relationship hasn't gone deeper.

Business Example: A colleague from a previous job who you enjoyed working with and would be happy to reconnect with, but with whom you haven't kept in touch.

Friend Example: Someone you know through mutual friends who you always enjoy talking to at gatherings, but with whom you've never made plans to hang out one-on-one.

★★☆☆☆ ACQUAINTANCES: THE FAMILIAR FACES

You've met. You might follow each other on social media. You'd recognize each other at an event. Like the person you see at your sister's barbecue every year—familiar, friendly, but no real depth.

Business Example: The person you met at a conference who you connected with on LinkedIn but haven't had any meaningful interaction with since.

Friend Example: Your neighbor, whom you wave to and make small talk with but whose life you don't know much about beyond surface-level details.

★☆☆☆☆ CONTACTS: NAMES IN YOUR PHONE

Business cards (or nowadays, the digital beaming of contacts we do with a quick tap). Social media connections. People you met once. People who exist in your network but you've never really connected with.

Business Example: The stack of business cards from the last networking event sitting in your desk drawer.

Friend Example: The person you met at a friend's party who you added on social media but haven't actually interacted with since.

Most people hoard contacts like trophies, thinking quantity equals influence. It doesn't. Relationship equity equals influence.

Component #2: Make Someone's Day—Your Daily Relationship Revolution

Once you understand the different levels in your network, you need a daily practice that ensures your good intentions become consistent action. This is where most people fail; they understand relationships matter, but they don't have a system for making relationship building happen consistently.

The Make Someone's Day Mindset is the single most powerful relationship-building tool you can implement.

Here's what it is. Wake up every morning with one question: *Who can I make smile today?*

Don't ask, *Who do I need to follow up with?* Not, *Who can help me with something?* Not, *Who owes me a response?*

Who can I make smile today?

This mindset shift changes everything. Instead of relationship building being something you do when you need something, it becomes something you do because you care about people. Instead of reaching out feeling transactional, it feels generous.

The 5x5 Method: Your Daily Practice

Before you check your first email, before you scroll social media, before you dive into your to-do list—implement what I call the 5x5 Method: Send five different types of messages to five people you care about, with the sole purpose of brightening their day.

The beauty of this approach is that you're reaching people across all levels of your network—from your closest advocates to valued connections—while varying your message types to keep it authentic and engaging. Here's how it works:

- **Message #1:** "I was just thinking about that project you mentioned last week. How's it coming along?"
- **Message #2:** A quick voice note: "Caught that song you love on the radio today—totally made me smile!"
- **Message #3:** A photo of that sunset from last week with the caption, "Reminded me of our conversation about slowing down."
- **Message #4:** An article share: "This made me think of the challenge you mentioned at coffee. Thought you might find it interesting."
- **Message #5:** A thirty-second video message: "Hey, just wanted you to know I'm rooting for you with that presentation today."

Five messages. Seven minutes total. Zero agenda except genuine care.

This mindset is revolutionary because it's completely unexpected. In a world where every message seems to want something, a message that just wants to brighten someone's day stands out like a beacon.

It's deeply personal. You're not broadcasting to your network; you're connecting one-on-one with specific people who matter to you. It creates emotional deposits. Every message builds goodwill, trust, and connection. You're investing in the relationship before you ever need to make a withdrawal. It shifts how people think about you. You become the person who shows up. The person who remembers. The person who cares enough to act on that care.

Here's what makes this so powerful: It feels completely spontaneous while being systematically consistent.

You're not following a script. You're not sending the same message to everyone. You're creating authentic moments of connection based on genuine thoughts and memories. But you're doing it every single day, which is what most people fail to do.

When someone gets a message from you because something reminded you of them—not because you need something, not only when it's their birthday, and not because you're launching something—it changes the entire dynamic of your relationship.

This is how you move from being someone in their network to being someone who matters in their life.

The Compound Effect of Daily Care

Here's what happens when you implement the 5x5 Method consistently.

Month One: By the end of the first month, people are surprised and delighted. You get responses like, "This made my day!" and "I was just thinking about you too!" They start to associate you with those positive feelings. You become the person who brightens their day just by showing up.

Months Three to Four: Your thoughtful presence sticks. People begin to reach out to you first when opportunities arise because you've been thinking of them consistently.

Month Six: Your relationships are deeper, your network is more responsive, and opportunities start coming to you instead of you having to chase them.

Year One: You've sent over eighteen hundred messages of genuine care. You've made someone's day more than eighteen hundred times. The compound effect of that consistency is impossible to replicate with sporadic interactions.

That kind of consistent care doesn't just build relationships; it transforms them. And the best part? It doesn't require chasing, pitching, or perfectly timed follow-ups. In fact, it's the opposite of traditional networking. Instead of reaching out when you need something, you reach out when you're thinking of someone. Instead of broadcasting your wins, you celebrate theirs. Instead of asking for introductions, you make them. Instead of promoting yourself, you promote others. This is what it looks like to create value before you ever ask for it. And that's what makes it work.

This approach works because it's built on genuine care, not strategic manipulation.

Making It Work in Your Real Life

Draw from your actual experiences. That coffee shop that reminded you of your conversation. The song that made you think of them. The article that connected to something they're working on.

Use whatever medium feels natural. Text, voice note, email, video message, handwritten note, social media comment; the medium doesn't matter as much as the intention.

Don't overthink it. "Thinking of you" is enough. "This made me smile and think of you" is perfect.

Be specific. Instead of "Hope you're doing well," try "Hope that new project is going better than you expected," or "Thinking about your presentation today."

Follow their lead. If they're a texter, text. If they love voice notes, send voice notes. If they're active on social media, comment on their posts or send them a DM.

The Mindset Shift That Changes Everything

The 5x5 Method isn't just about sending messages; it's about training yourself to think generously about the people in your life.

When you wake up asking, *Who can I make smile today?* you start noticing opportunities to add value everywhere.

- You start remembering important events in people's lives.
- You celebrate others' wins genuinely.
- You offer to help before being asked.
- You make introductions that benefit others.
- You share opportunities that aren't right for you but are perfect for someone else.

This mindset creates a reputation that money can't buy—being someone who genuinely cares about others' success.

Component #3: The Frequency Formula—Preventing Relationship Drift

Once you understand your relationship levels and have a daily practice for consistent connection, you need strategic timing to ensure relationships don't drift away from neglect.

The relationships that matter most require consistent investment. But "consistent" doesn't mean "constant." It means strategic and sustainable.

Here's the frequency formula I use that prevents relationships from drifting away. It's not a rule set in stone, but it is a starting point you can adapt to fit your style and needs.

- Advocates (★★★★★): Every 30 days
- Champions (★★★★☆): Every 60 days
- Connections (★★★☆☆): Every 90 days
- Acquaintances (★★☆☆☆): Every 120 days
- Contacts (★☆☆☆☆): Database, mailing list touchpoints, or just contacts you keep

Why These Intervals Work

Advocates (30 Days): Your most important relationships need the most consistent investment. Monthly contact keeps you top of mind and maintains the advocacy momentum.

Champions (60 Days): Regular enough to stay connected, spaced enough to avoid being overwhelming. This interval maintains the relationship without feeling forced.

Connections (90 Days): Quarterly contact maintains the relationship and creates opportunities for it to deepen naturally. It's the sweet spot between staying connected and giving space.

Acquaintances (120 Days): Just often enough to prevent complete drift while being realistic about investment capacity.

Contacts (Variable): Group communication—newsletters, updates, social media. Mass communication that keeps the door open without individual investment.

This formula is a starting point, not a rule. Adjust based on some of the following factors:

- **Life Events:** Someone going through a transition might need more frequent contact temporarily.
- **Personality Types:** Some people prefer less frequent but deeper contact.

- **Mutual Preferences:** Some relationships naturally have different rhythms.
- **Seasons:** Business relationships might need different frequency during peak seasons.
- **Geography:** Long-distance relationships might need more frequent digital contact.

The goal isn't to turn relationships into spreadsheet entries. It's to ensure that good intentions become consistent actions. The system serves the relationship, not the other way around.

Component #4: The Power of a Handwritten Note

In a world where we receive hundreds of digital messages daily, there's one form of communication that stops people in their tracks: a handwritten note.

I learned this lesson early in my real estate career when I started sending handwritten thank-you notes to clients. Not just after every transaction closed, but after listing appointments, buyer consultations, and thoughtful moments throughout our relationship. When clients did something nice for me, when I was simply thinking about them, or when something reminded me of our conversations—I'd put pen to paper.

These weren't printed cards with my logo plastered all over them. Not generic "thank you for your business" templates. They were actual handwritten notes on quality cards with personal messages that referenced specific moments from our time working together.

The response was immediate and unforgettable. Clients would call me weeks later just to tell me how much that note meant to them. They'd show it to their friends. Some even framed them. One client told me she kept my note on her refrigerator for two years because it made her smile every time she saw it.

But here's what really opened my eyes: Those handwritten notes generated more referrals than any other marketing effort I'd ever tried. Not because they were a marketing tactic, but because they *weren't*. They were genuine expressions of gratitude and connection that made people feel truly valued.

Why Handwritten Notes Are Neurological Gold

There's actual science behind why handwritten notes create such powerful responses. When someone receives a handwritten note, their brain processes it differently than digital communication. The tactile experience of holding paper, seeing the slight imperfections in handwriting, and feeling the texture of the stationery—all of this creates a deeper sensory experience.

Your brain recognizes that someone took time, effort, and physical energy to create something just for you. The physical act of handwriting engages different cognitive processes than typing, leading to stronger emotional connections and memory formation. When someone receives your handwritten note, they're not just reading your words—they're experiencing your investment of time and attention.

In our digital world, handwritten notes have become even more powerful because they're increasingly rare. Studies show that the average person receives fewer than five handwritten notes per year outside of holiday cards. This means your handwritten note doesn't just stand out—it's a quiet impact that speaks volumes.

The Strategic Timing of Handwritten vs. Digital

Not every communication should be handwritten, but knowing when to choose pen over pixel can transform the impact of your relationship building.

Here are the best opportunities to use handwritten notes to connect:

- Expressing gratitude for something significant
- Acknowledging a major life event (promotion, birth, marriage, loss)
- Following up after an important meeting or conversation
- Apologizing for a mistake or misunderstanding
- Celebrating someone's achievement
- Sending condolences or support during difficult times

Stick with digital when you're:

- Sharing quick updates or information
- Coordinating logistics or schedules
- Responding to immediate questions
- Sending resources or links
- Managing day-to-day business communications

The rule of thumb: If the message could change how someone feels about themselves or their relationship with you, consider handwritten. If it's purely informational, digital is fine.

Handwritten Note Scenarios That Open Doors

The Gratitude Follow-Up: After a networking event or meaningful conversation, consider a statement like this one: "Thank you for taking the time to share your insights about the healthcare industry with me yesterday. Your perspective on patient advocacy really resonated with me, and I've been thinking about our conversation ever since."

The Achievement Celebration: When someone in your network has a win, consider this statement: "Saw the announcement about your promotion to regional director. Knowing how hard you've worked and how much you care about your team, this couldn't have happened to a more deserving person."

The Thoughtful Check-In: When someone in your inner or outer circle is going through something challenging, consider this: "I know this month marks one year since your dad passed away. I've been thinking about you and wanted you to know that his kindness and wisdom clearly live on in you."

The Introduction Follow-Up: After making a new connection, try this messaging: "It was such a pleasure introducing you to Sarah last week. She mentioned you two have already had a great conversation about potential collaboration. I love when connections I make turn into something meaningful."

The System That Preserves Authenticity

The key to making handwritten notes a consistent part of your relationship building—without losing their personal touch—is preparation, not automation. I keep a basket on my desk stocked with everything I need: quality notecards, stamps, and my favorite colored markers, so there's zero friction when inspiration strikes.

But it's not just about having the supplies—it's about being mindful of the moments that matter. I pay attention to the little cues: after a meaningful meeting or conversation, when I see someone celebrate a big win on social media, during life milestones like graduations or anniversaries, or even when someone simply does something kind that impacts me or my business. I also make sure to reach out during the hard seasons when people need encouragement the most. These aren't scheduled tasks—they're intentional moments that remind me to pause, pick up a pen, and let someone know they matter.

While every note should feel personal, having a loose structure helps you write more efficiently:

1. Acknowledge the specific moment or achievement.
2. Appreciate something about them or their impact.
3. Connect it to a broader truth about who they are.
4. Close with genuine warmth.

Making this a priority matters; just schedule fifteen minutes twice a week for handwritten notes. This small time investment—thirty minutes total—can typically produce four to six thoughtful notes that will create relationship dividends for months or years to come.

One last thing: Handwritten notes only work if they're real. If you don't mean it, don't write it. Reference specific details to show you were truly present. Use your natural voice—whether that's warm and casual or more polished and professional. And most importantly, don't rush. If you're in a hurry, wait. These notes aren't about checking a box. They're about creating connection. And connection deserves your full attention.

What makes handwritten notes so powerful in relationship building isn't just their rarity—it's their permanence. Digital messages get deleted, archived, or lost in the flood of daily communication. But handwritten notes often get kept, displayed, or treasured.

I've been in clients' homes years after our real estate transaction and seen my handwritten thank-you note still posted on their refrigerator. I've had business partners reference handwritten condolence notes

I sent during family losses, telling me how much that small gesture meant during their darkest days.

This is the compound effect of analog care in a digital world. When you take the time to put pen to paper, you're not just sending a message—you're creating a physical reminder that someone matters to you. You're building relationship equity that appreciates over time.

The most successful relationship builders I know aren't necessarily the most naturally gifted writers or the most technologically savvy. They're the ones who understand that in our hyperconnected, always-on world, sometimes the most powerful way to connect is to slow down, pick up a pen, and write something meaningful by hand.

Because in the end, relationships aren't built on efficiency—they're built on intention. And nothing communicates intention quite like taking the time to write someone a note they'll want to keep forever.

Component #5: The Moment-Based Touch Strategy

While the frequency formula gives you the foundation for consistent relationship maintenance, the most powerful relationship builders know how to layer in additional touches based on life's meaningful moments. These aren't scheduled contacts; they're opportunities that present themselves when you're paying attention.

The difference between good relationship builders and great ones isn't just consistency—it's timing. Great relationship builders show up at the moments that matter most.

But here's the crucial truth: The moments that matter won't raise their hands.

They don't announce themselves with flashing lights. They slip by quietly in casual conversations, social media posts, and offhand comments. The promotion someone's nervous about. The anniversary of a loss. The kid who's starting kindergarten. The presentation that's keeping them up at night. The medical procedure they are having next month.

Most people miss these moments entirely because they're not listening for them. But when you catch them—when you show up at exactly the right time—you create relationship magic that lasts for years.

Here's what most people get wrong: They think only the big moments matter. The wedding, the promotion, the new baby. But relationships are built in the accumulation of smaller moments—the Tuesday when someone mentions feeling overwhelmed, the casual comment about their teenager struggling in school, and the excitement in their voice when they talk about a new project.

Every interaction is a chance to make a deposit in your relationship account. Every moment of genuine care compounds over time. The question isn't whether moments matter—it's whether you're intentional enough to recognize and act on them.

The Two Types of Relationship Moments

Calendar Moments: These are the predictable dates you can plan for—birthdays, work anniversaries, holidays, and graduations. While they're scheduled, they still require intentionality. Most people forget these dates or send generic, last-minute messages. Being thoughtful and timely with calendar moments already puts you ahead of 90 percent of people.

Life Moments: These are the unpredictable events that reveal who's really paying attention—promotions, job changes, family additions, health challenges, personal victories, or losses. These moments are relationship gold because most people miss them entirely.

Your Moment Recognition System

Social Media Monitoring: Make it a habit to check Instagram, Facebook, and LinkedIn with relationship-building eyes. When you're scrolling, you're looking for moments—not just entertainment. When someone posts about a promotion, new job, family milestone, or personal achievement, being among the first to acknowledge it creates exponentially more impact than a generic "congrats" much later.

The Important Date Tracker: Beyond birthdays, track the dates that matter to them: their work anniversary, their kids' birthdays, the anniversary of a parent's passing, and their wedding anniversary. Put these in your calendar with reminders. These show you're not just remembering obvious dates—you're remembering their life.

The Listening Loop: When people share what's coming up in their lives—"Nick starts college in the fall." "We're launching the new product line in March." "My dad's surgery is next Tuesday."—immediately put these in your calendar with reminders to follow up. Most people share these details, but few people remember to check back in.

Taking Action: Beyond the Message

The key is matching your response to the significance of the moment. Not every occasion calls for the same level of investment, but every moment deserves intentional acknowledgment:

Phone Calls for Major Moments: When someone gets a big promotion, experiences a loss, or hits a major milestone, pick up the phone. Your voice conveys emotion and presence that text can't match. "I had to call because I'm so excited for you" carries weight that no emoji can replicate.

Handwritten Notes: For lasting impact, significant achievements, difficult times, or moments you want them to remember, handwritten notes create permanence. They get kept, displayed, and treasured in ways digital messages never will.

Thoughtful Gifts and Surprises: Sometimes the moment calls for something tangible. Their favorite coffee delivered to their office on a stressful day. A book that relates to something they're working through. Flowers for their big presentation day. The gesture doesn't have to be expensive—it just has to show you were thinking about them.

The Power of Handwritten Birthday Cards: In a world of Facebook birthday notifications and text messages, a handwritten birthday card stops people in their tracks. It requires planning, intention, and personal investment. I've had clients frame birthday cards I've sent them because they're so rare and meaningful. The card itself becomes a gift—a tangible reminder that they matter enough for you to plan ahead and write something personal.

Moment-Based Response Examples

The Day-Before Call: "I wanted to call because I know tomorrow is Nick's first day of college. How are you holding up?"

The Celebration Gift: Sending their favorite lunch to the office after their big presentation with a note: "Knew you'd nail it. Celebrate yourself today!"

The Anniversary Note: A handwritten card acknowledging the anniversary of a parent's passing: "Thinking of you today and remembering how proud your dad would be of who you've become."

The Milestone Surprise: Flowers delivered for their work anniversary with a card: "Ten years of making a difference. Here's to many more!"

Making It Systematic Without Losing Heart

Use technology to remember, but always respond personally:

- Schedule regular social media check-ins with relationship-building intent.
- Use calendar reminders for important upcoming dates.
- Keep a running note in your phone of things people mention.
- Stock up on note cards and small gifts so you're ready when moments arise.
- But always craft personal, specific responses that show you were truly listening.

The moment-based strategy doesn't replace your frequency formula—it enhances it. You're still maintaining regular contact, but you're also showing up at the times when your presence means the most.

Because in the end, people don't just remember that you showed up consistently. They remember that you showed up when it mattered. And the moments that matter most are often the ones that slip by unnoticed unless you're intentionally watching for them.

How Relationships Drift—and How to Stop It

Relationships don't die from conflict—they drift away from neglect. Relationship drift happens gradually, then suddenly. You mean to call. You plan to reach out. Life gets busy. Time passes. Before you know it, reaching out feels awkward because it's been too long.

The Warning Signs of Drift

Conversations become purely transactional.

- You only hear from them when they need something (or vice versa).
- Social media becomes your primary connection point.
- You think about reaching out but don't follow through.
- When you do connect, you spend time "catching up" on basic life updates.

The Recovery Strategy

When drift has already happened (and it will), here's how to rebuild:

- **Acknowledge honestly:** "I realized it's been way too long since we connected, and that's on me."
- **Take responsibility:** "I've been terrible at staying in touch."
- **Express genuine care:** "You've been on my mind, and I wanted to reach out."
- **Make it about them:** "How are you? Really—not just the highlight reel."
- **Commit to consistency:** "I don't want to let this much time pass again."

Most people are gracious about drift when you own it and show genuine interest in reconnecting.

Tools That Support (Don't Replace) Connection

While nothing can replace genuine human connection, using the right tools helps you stay organized and intentional in maintaining your relationships. These tools aren't a substitute for authentic interaction; they're your helpers, keeping you on track so you don't let important connections slip through the cracks.

- **Customer Relationship Management (CRM) or Contact Management Systems:** Help you track the last time you connected and remind you when to reach out next so no relationship goes neglected.
- **Calendar Reminders:** Treat relationship maintenance like any other critical task by scheduling regular check-ins and follow-ups.
- **Note-Taking System:** Capture personal details, conversation highlights, and key dates to personalize your outreach and show you truly listen.
- **Photo/Video Tools:** Make it easy to share memories, celebrate milestones, or send quick, meaningful messages that keep connections vibrant.

Used thoughtfully, these tools empower you to build a relationship system that's both scalable and deeply personal.

The Authenticity Balance

The question always comes up: "Doesn't this make relationships feel calculated?"

Here's the truth: Intention isn't manipulation when it comes from genuine care. You already prioritize what matters to you. You schedule time for work projects, fitness goals, and family commitments. Why wouldn't you be equally intentional about the relationships that create the foundation for everything else in your life?

The system doesn't create fake relationships—it ensures that your genuine care translates into consistent action.

I also often hear, "This all sounds great, but I haven't been in touch with people in months (or years). Isn't it too late? Won't it be awkward?"

My answer is simple: "Just start. Rip the Band-Aid off. Don't apologize."

Stop overthinking it. Stop making it complicated. Stop letting perfect be the enemy of good.

You know what's more awkward than reaching out after a long silence? Never reaching out at all.

You know what's worse than a relationship that's been dormant? A relationship that's completely dead.

The best time to start building intentional relationships was five years ago. The second-best time is right now.

Don't lead with apologies. "I'm so sorry I haven't been in touch" immediately makes the conversation about your failure instead of about them.

Don't make excuses. "I've been so busy" is what everyone says. It's not interesting or meaningful.

Don't make it about the gap. "I know it's been forever" draws attention to the exact thing you're trying to move past.

Instead, just start. Consider some of these options:

"Saw this article about remote work trends and thought of our conversation about the future of offices. How are you adapting to everything?"

"This song came on the radio and reminded me of your terrible taste in music. Hope you're crushing it at the new job."

"Been thinking about that advice you gave me about difficult conversations. It's made a huge difference. How are things going with you?"

When you think of someone you haven't talked to in a while, you have twenty-four hours to reach out. After that, you'll talk yourself out of it. We've all experienced this: "I should reach out to Jennifer" becomes "I'll do it after this meeting" becomes "It's been so long it would be awkward." The solution is simple: When you think of someone, reach out within twenty-four hours. Don't overthink it, don't craft the perfect message, just reach out.

Lead with value. Lead with care. Lead with genuine interest in their life. When you just start, without the drama, most people are gracious. They're happy to hear from you and don't need a detailed explanation of why you haven't been in touch. The awkwardness exists mostly in your head. What feels massive to you feels normal to them.

Relationships pick up faster than you think. Good relationships have elasticity—they can stretch and then snap back into place. Action creates momentum. The hardest part is sending that first message. After that, it gets easier.

The Truth About Relationship Systems

Here's what I want you to understand: You already have a relationship system. The question is whether it's serving you or failing you. If you're constantly playing catch-up with people who matter to you, if opportunities come as surprises instead of natural outcomes, or if you feel disconnected despite having a large network—your current system isn't working.

If people aren't coming back to you in business and if they're calling other professionals to help them, leaving you thinking, *That should have been me*—your current system isn't working.

The choice isn't between authentic relationships and systematic ones. The choice is between intentional relationships and accidental ones.

The Relationship Operating System doesn't create fake connections—it ensures that your genuine care translates into consistent action. It doesn't make relationships transactional—it makes relationship building sustainable.

Because at the end of the day, the relationships that change your life aren't built in moments of inspiration. They're built in moments of consistency.

PART III

Relationships That Make an Impact

CHAPTER 11

Everyone's in Sales: The Powerful Truth About Influence

Before you skip this chapter thinking it doesn't apply to you, consider this: When did you last convince someone to see your point of view? When did you last persuade, influence, or inspire someone to take action? If you've done any of those things, you're already in sales—whether you realize it or not.

Think about it: Convincing your toddler to tie their shoes is sales. Persuading the hostess to give you that table by the window so you can watch the sunset is sales. Getting your teenager to clean their room, or negotiating with your spouse about weekend plans—it's all sales.

But it's also negotiating a contract with a vendor, presenting a proposal to the board, convincing your team to embrace a new process, or inspiring stakeholders to approve your budget. Sales is influence, and we are all influencing others every single day, both personally and professionally.

The moment you try to move someone from where they are to where you want them to be, you're selling. The question isn't whether you're in sales—it's whether you're good at it. And being good at it starts with understanding that sales isn't about manipulation or pressure tactics. It's about relationships.

And here's the critical truth: Anyone who touches the client or customer is in sales. Your receptionist answering the phone, your billing department handling payment issues, your customer service team resolving problems—they're all selling. With every interaction, they're either building the relationship or eroding it.

This is why it's crucial that everyone on your team adopts these relationship principles, not just the people with "sales" in their job titles.

The companies that truly understand the relationship advantage train their entire team in these principles. They recognize that a single negative touchpoint can undo months of relationship building, while a single exceptional moment can create a customer for life.

The Relationship Trigger System

Let me give you a real-world example: Your receptionist reschedules an appointment because someone's grandmother passed away. In a transactional business, that's the end of the interaction. In a relationship-focused business, that receptionist triggers a system—flowers get sent, a personal note is written, and when the client returns, everyone on the team knows to express condolences.

Think about the impact: The client is dealing with grief, and your business responds with genuine care. Which company do you think they'll remember? Which company do you think they'll recommend when someone asks for a referral?

When your entire team embraces relationship principles, there's a positive compounding impact on relationships and the business.

- Customer service becomes customer success. Problems become opportunities to demonstrate care.
- Billing becomes relationship maintenance. Payment issues are handled with empathy and understanding.
- Reception becomes the first impression. Every phone call and greeting builds trust.
- Operations becomes relationship protection. Every process is designed with the customer experience in mind.
- Problem resolution becomes relationship strengthening. How you handle issues defines the relationship more than how you handle success.

The most successful businesses I know have systems that ensure every team member can contribute to the relationship advantage. They train everyone to recognize relationship-building moments and empower them to act on them. Because in the end, your customers aren't just buying from you; they're buying from your entire organization. Make sure everyone is selling relationships, not just transactions.

The Six-Pound Awakening

When I first started in real estate sales, I was handed what my manager called "the formula for success." It was a script, a clipboard, and zero training. I was told to go out and "knock on doors," and at every door, it was the same thing:

Knock, knock, knock. "Have you thought about selling your home?"

The door slammed in my face.

Next door. *Knock, knock, knock.* "Have you thought about selling your home?"

The door slammed in my face.

One day, I was walking down a tree-lined street in Lakewood, California, when I approached a house with one of those old aluminum screen doors—you know the kind, mesh on top, metal on the bottom, with a push-button handle. The second I knocked on this particular door, I could hear it rattle, and I immediately thought, *This door isn't latched all the way.*

Then I heard the noise—a very angry noise—come running toward the door. I instinctively knew it was a dog, and this dog was not stopping. So yes, you guessed it, I ran off the porch and down the street. Thank goodness there was a gardener tending to a lawn nearby who helped scare that beast back to its home.

Now, before we move on, what kind of dog are you picturing? A giant, beastly German shepherd or pit bull, right?

Well, no. A six-pound Chihuahua changed the trajectory of my sales career forever.

After I caught my breath—palms sweating, still shaking—I went and sat in my car and had a conversation with myself. I didn't sign up for this. I didn't sign up to get yelled at or to have doors slammed in my face, and I certainly didn't sign up to get chased by a dog. I signed up to help people.

And that's when I realized I was doing this business all wrong. I was chasing transactions instead of building relationships.

The Technology Trap

After that revelation, I was given what I thought was the "gift" of technology. I'll never forget the day I was called into my sales manager's office and he said, "Barb, would you be interested in being the first platform agent in our office?"

My first thought was, *What is a platform agent?*

I quickly learned that Prudential California Realty would be the first firm to receive brand-new internet leads, hosted and distributed through real estate searches on Yahoo.com. (Side note: This was the first version of the real estate internet portals you're so used to now.) I immediately said yes, thinking, *This will be the answer!*

Before I knew it, I was responding to leads coming from Yahoo. They were warmer than cold calls, at least. People had clicked on something that showed interest in buying a home, so they were already halfway there.

But it wasn't the answer I thought it would be. I sat there responding to emails and calling people who still felt like strangers. Sure, they had shown some interest, but they weren't my people. I still felt disconnected, like I was just reading a script—because I was—only this time, it was in digital form.

The company had provided us with template responses for different scenarios:

"Thank you for your interest in real estate! I'd love to schedule a time to discuss your home-buying needs. When would be convenient for you?"

"I see you're interested in homes in the three hundred thousand to four hundred thousand range. I have several properties that might be perfect for you. Can we set up some showings this weekend?"

Even my phone calls followed a prescribed format: introduce yourself, thank them for their inquiry, ask qualifying questions about their timeline and budget, then push for an appointment. It was efficient, but it felt hollow. The words didn't really connect with anyone—because they weren't my words, and they certainly weren't tailored to who these people actually were or what they truly needed.

It felt like I was still knocking on doors, only now it was via email.

And that's when I realized the trap I'd fallen into.

I'd assumed that because someone clicked a link or filled out a form, the relationship had already begun. I mistook digital interest for genuine connection. But a lead isn't a relationship. A name in your inbox isn't trust. Templates and scripts might save time, but they can't replace the groundwork of truly getting to know someone—their story, their goals, their fears, their "why."

Technology can open the door, but it can't walk through it for you. The real work still happens in the human moments—when you ask questions that matter, listen for what's unsaid, and show you understand what they actually want.

It wasn't until I stopped focusing on the immediate sale and started thinking about the relationship that I began to see real results. I realized the tech wasn't the answer—it was the relationship that would drive success.

The Transactional Trap

In business, we get so caught up in hitting numbers, closing deals, and moving on to the next one that it's easy to forget the most important part of what we're doing—relationships. The real success comes not from chasing the next sale but from nurturing the relationships that last. Yet so many of us, myself included in the beginning, get stuck in what I call the *transactional trap*.

Transactional sales might help you close deals, but they're not the foundation of long-term success. Sure, you can measure how many deals you close, how much revenue you generate, and how fast you move on to the next one, but those numbers don't tell you anything about trust. They don't tell you anything about loyalty. And without trust, there's no long-term success.

In those early days, I was so focused on closing the next deal that

I wasn't paying attention to the real heart of the process: the relationship with my client. I was chasing after sales like that six-pound Chihuahua chasing me off the porch—lots of noise and energy, but not much substance.

Transactional sales might get you quick wins, but they won't create loyal clients or lasting partnerships. They don't build trust. And without trust, there's no long-term success.

Here's what I learned the hard way: People don't do business with numbers; people do business with people.

Transactional business may be trackable.
But it's not transformational.

When you focus solely on the transaction, you lose sight of what really matters—the relationship. You might hit your targets in the short term, but you'll never get the deep, loyal clients who trust you, refer you, and come back to you time and time again. It's the relationships that will sustain you through tough times, not the quick wins.

THE TALE OF TWO APPROACHES

Transactional Sales	Relational Sales
Cold Calls and Door-Knocking: Chasing numbers rather than connections, focusing on quantity over quality.	**Building Trust over Time:** Focusing on understanding the client's needs and creating a long-term relationship.
Scripted Interactions: Using rigid scripts with little room for personalization, ensuring the process follows a set formula.	**Personalized Conversations:** Listening first and having flexible, natural conversations that address the client's specific needs.

Transactional Sales	Relational Sales
One-Time Deals: The goal is simply to close the sale, with no focus on ongoing engagement or future opportunities.	**Repeat Business and Referrals:** Emphasizing the long-term relationship, ensuring clients return and refer others.
Impersonal Communications: Relying on automated responses, generic email blasts, and AI-driven messaging that lack personal touch.	**Authentic, Human Communication:** Sending personalized, thoughtful messages that reflect genuine care and concern.
Chasing Sales Metrics: Focusing solely on hitting sales quotas, closing rates, and the number of transactions closed.	**Focused on Long-Term Success:** Measuring success by the depth of client relationships and their continued success, not just the quantity of sales.
Minimal Follow-Up: Once the deal is done, moving on to the next lead without checking in or maintaining the relationship.	**Ongoing Engagement:** Continuing to engage with clients after the sale, offering value, and maintaining a strong, consistent relationship.

The Relationship Trifecta: Your Business Lifeline

Now let's talk about what really matters in business and sales: repeat business, retention, and referrals. These aren't just buzzwords or strategies—they're the lifeblood of any sustainable business. This relationship trifecta is what creates long-term success. And at the heart of it all? Relationships. Real, consistent, trust-filled relationships that keep people coming back, sticking around, and telling others about you.

Repeat Business: When Clients Choose You Again

When you build strong relationships, you create repeat business. When you genuinely care for your clients and show them that you are there for the long haul, they come back to you when they need something else. They don't shop around because they already trust you. They don't compare prices because they know you'll take care of them.

Repeat business is about being the first call when a new need arises. You may not work together every day, but when the moment comes—when a client is ready to buy, sell, or start again—they come back to you because the relationship hasn't faded.

Your consistency, follow-through, and genuine care earn you the privilege of serving them again and again, even across seasons or life changes.

Retention: The Power of Loyalty

People stay with you when they feel valued. When you've established a real connection with someone, when you've built a relationship that's rooted in trust, they're not going anywhere. Retention is about ongoing partnership—the kind that renews itself every month, year, or cycle because the relationship is active and alive. Think of it as a continuous commitment: insurance clients who keep paying premiums, service members who stay subscribed, and customers who see you as indispensable.

They'll stay loyal to you because they know you're someone they can count on. And when you deliver consistent value, they don't just stay—they deepen their investment in you.

Retention isn't just about keeping customers—it's about creating advocates. Loyal clients don't just stay; they become your biggest cheerleaders, your word-of-mouth marketers, and your business partners in growth.

Referrals: Your Clients Become Your Sales Team

This is where relationships really shine. The thing that every business owner and every salesperson is striving for. When you've built trust with your clients, they'll refer you to their family and friends—to people they know and care about. You don't have to ask for referrals; they come to you because you've shown up for your clients time and time again. You've proven yourself worthy of their trust.

Think about it: When someone refers you to their family, they're putting their own reputation on the line. They're saying, "I trust this person so much that I'm willing to stake my relationship with you on their performance." That's not something people do lightly.

The moment I stopped chasing transactions and started focusing on relationships, I saw the real power of this trifecta. I started building trust with clients, and as a result, they came back, referred me to others, and stayed loyal to me.

The Trust Bridge

People don't do business with you until they know you, like you, and finally trust you. Trust is the bridge that turns a transaction into a lasting connection.

Trust is what makes the difference between a one-time sale and a lifelong client. Trust is what makes the difference between a cold call and a meaningful relationship. Trust is what transforms a skeptical prospect into a raving fan.

When you build relationships, you build trust. And when you build trust, you create a sustainable, thriving business that isn't dependent on the next sale or the next deal. You create a foundation that stands the test of time, regardless of what happens in the market or the economy.

But here's what most people get wrong about trust: Trust isn't built in big moments—it's built in small, consistent actions. It's built in the follow-up call you make just to check in. It's built in the birthday card you send. It's built in the way you handle problems when they arise. It's built into the referral you give them when they need something you don't provide.

Trust is earned in drops and lost in buckets. Every interaction either builds trust or erodes it. There's no neutral ground.

And yet, here's where most relationship-building advice falls short: It tells you to "build relationships" without explaining what makes those relationships actually work.

Because sales is more than relationships; it's about the trust and value *inside* those relationships.

You can have warm, friendly relationships with hundreds of people and still struggle to generate referrals. Why? Because a relationship alone isn't enough. What matters is whether that relationship carries two things: trust and demonstrated value.

Trust means they believe you'll deliver on your promises and act in their best interest. It's not just liking you—it's having confidence that you'll show up and follow through.

Value means they've seen what you can do. They've experienced the way you solve problems or make their life measurably better. It's not just being helpful—it's being consistently excellent.

Think about the people you refer to others—your doctor, your accountant, your favorite restaurant. You don't refer them just because you know them. You refer them because you trust them completely and you've experienced their value firsthand.

The relationship gets you in the door.

The trust gets you the referral.

The value gets you the advocacy.

Together, they create the kind of business that sustains itself through any market condition.

The Human vs. Machine Dilemma

In today's fast-paced world, technology has become a fundamental part of sales. We've swapped cold-calling and door-knocking for automated emails, AI chatbots, and marketing funnels. It's easy to see why: Automation speeds up the process, AI makes it scalable, and funnels are designed to convert leads quickly. It's an approach that promises efficiency—but at what cost?

It's true, automation and AI have revolutionized sales. With just a few clicks, we can send thousands of messages, track engagement, and measure conversion rates. We can use AI to predict customer behavior and personalize outreach, all without lifting a finger. And let's be honest, it feels a lot easier than walking door-to-door or dialing random numbers.

Technology has certainly made our lives easier, but here's the critical question: Has it made us better at building relationships?

AI can write emails, analyze data, and even respond to questions through chatbots, but it can't truly connect with people. Automation is fast, but it's impersonal.

Think about the last time you received an email from a company that was clearly a template or a bot-generated response. It felt robotic, right? It was missing the human touch. You could tell it was automated. Sure, it might have had your name in the subject line and maybe even some personalized recommendations based on previous purchases, but it lacked the authenticity of a real person who cared about your needs.

Let's talk about funnels for a moment. Sales funnels are designed to take a lead through a series of steps, from awareness to decision-making, with the goal of turning that lead into a paying customer. The problem with funnels is that they treat people like numbers—steps in a process rather than individuals with unique needs and emotions.

Funnels work great for measuring conversions and making sales predictions, but they don't take the time to build trust or create long-term relationships. Funnels treat prospects as one-size-fits-all, guiding them through a predetermined path that leads to a sale, with very little room for genuine connection or personalization.

Funnels are designed for speed, but relationships are built over time. People don't feel valued when they're funneled through an automated system that treats them like a number. And without trust, those clients are unlikely to return for repeat business or refer others to you.

The Integration Solution

Here's the thing: I'm not anti-technology. In fact, I use AI daily in my business—and you should too. AI is incredibly powerful for handling the tasks that don't require human connection but eat up valuable time.

Here are some of the tasks I rely on AI to help me with:

- Draft initial email responses that I then personalize.
- Analyze client data to identify patterns and opportunities.
- Create social media content calendars and post ideas.
- Transcribe and summarize client calls so I can focus on listening instead of note-taking.
- Research prospects before meetings so I can ask better questions.
- Generate follow-up task lists and reminders.
- Write first drafts of proposals that I then customize for each client.

Technology is a powerful tool that can enhance relationships when used correctly. The key is to use technology to support human connection, not replace it. AI can help you be more prepared, more organized, and more responsive—but it can never replace the moment when you look a client in the eye and truly understand their fear, their hope, or their dream.

But never forget that at the end of the day, people want to do business with people, not machines. They want to feel seen, heard, and valued. They want to know that there's a real person who cares about their success and their satisfaction.

The Power of Influence Over Sales

Here's what I discovered after years of chasing transactions: Influence is more scalable than sales. One sale closes one deal. One act of influence starts a ripple effect.

Think about it: When you pressure someone into a purchase, that transaction ends with the signature. But when you influence someone—when you genuinely help them see a better path forward—that impact travels. It spreads through word of mouth, social media, shared stories, testimonials, and transformed lives. Influence multiplies because it resonates. It grows because it's authentic.

This is why the most successful salespeople I know stopped thinking of themselves as salespeople and started thinking of themselves as influencers. They don't just close deals; they shift perspectives. They don't just hit quotas; they create movements among their client base.

When you focus on influence instead of sales:

- People share your message instead of avoiding your calls.
- Clients become advocates instead of one-time buyers.

- Your reputation precedes you instead of your pitch.
- Referrals flow naturally instead of being forced.
- Trust builds systematically instead of being manufactured.

Remember that six-pound Chihuahua that chased me off the porch? I was trying to sell. The homeowner was resisting. And in that moment, everything felt like a failure. But sometimes, it's the smallest moments—the ones that seem insignificant at the time—that end up shaping everything. That day didn't lead to a sale, but it did lead to a shift. A new perspective. A turning point in how I approached people, not just transactions.

If you want to increase your sales,
you need to increase your *influence*.

If you lead with sales, people will resist. If you lead with influence, people will respond.

Whether you're in business, leadership, or everyday life—your ability to influence will determine your impact. Start here:

- Share stories, not just features. People don't buy products; they buy better versions of themselves. Paint the picture of their transformed life.
- Ask more questions than you give answers. The person asking questions controls the conversation. More importantly, questions show you care about their situation, not just your commission.
- Listen deeply before you lead boldly. You can't influence someone's thinking until you understand their current perspective. Listen for the real problem behind their stated need.

- Care before you convince. Genuine concern can't be faked, and people can sense it immediately. When they feel your authentic care, resistance melts away.

People don't remember pitches. They remember how you made them feel. And when someone feels seen, valued, and believed in—they'll follow you without needing to be "sold."

This is the real secret behind the relationship advantage: It's not about better sales techniques. It's about becoming someone worth following, someone whose influence naturally attracts the right people at the right time.

If you implement the strategies learned from the Relationship Operating System in chapter 10 and apply the principles you've learned throughout this book, whether it's shifting from transactional to relational sales, focusing on trust and loyalty, or embracing technology to enhance human connection, you can completely transform your sales career, just like I did.

When I first started, I was focused on hitting numbers, closing deals, and moving to the next one. But once I made the shift to prioritizing relationships, everything changed. Not only did my approach become more authentic and fulfilling, but I also started seeing results that were sustainable and long-lasting. I moved from chasing sales to building meaningful connections that created loyalty, trust, and, most importantly, long-term success.

The Compound Effect of Relational Sales

Here's what happened when I started prioritizing relationships over sales:

Year One: I closed fewer deals but built deeper relationships. My income actually dipped slightly, but my stress levels plummeted. I was no longer dreading Monday mornings.

Year Two: The referrals started flowing. Former clients began recommending me to their friends and family. My conversion rates on new leads increased dramatically because I was being referred by people who trusted me.

Year Three: I was working with second- and third-generation clients. People who had bought their first home with me were now buying their dream home. Others were selling and buying again. The lifetime value of my clients skyrocketed.

Year Five: I had built a business that sustained itself. I was no longer dependent on generating new leads because my existing network was generating them for me. I was working less but earning more because I was working with people who already trusted me.

Year Ten and Beyond: This is where the real magic of relationships revealed itself. I've now lived through multiple economic downturns, market crashes, and yes, even the Great Recession—the biggest housing recession in history. While other agents were struggling to survive, scrambling for leads, and leaving the industry entirely, my business remained stable.

Why? Because relationships transcend economies.

When the market crashed in 2008, I didn't lose clients—I helped them navigate the crisis. When people were underwater on their mortgages, I wasn't just their agent; I was their trusted advisor helping them make difficult decisions. When the market was uncertain, they didn't shop around for different representation; they leaned on the relationship we'd built over years.

During every recession I've weathered, the same pattern emerged: Transaction-focused agents disappeared, but relationship-focused agents endured. When people are scared, when money is tight, and when the future feels uncertain, they don't want to work with strangers—they want to work with people they trust.

The relationships I had built became my recession-proof foundation. Past clients still needed to move, downsize, or make strategic decisions. They still referred friends and family members who needed guidance. The difference was that in good times, relationships gave me an advantage. In tough times, relationships gave me survival.

This is the ultimate compound effect of relational sales: You don't just build a business that thrives in good markets; you build a business that endures through any economic climate.

The truth is that sales is not about closing deals—it's about building relationships. When you invest in the people you serve, when you listen, build trust, and consistently show up for them, the sales will follow. The relationships you create will carry you through the toughest times and keep you growing for years to come.

Here's what I wish someone had told me on that first day when I was handed a clipboard and a script: You're not just selling a product or a service—you're selling yourself. Make those connections count.

Influence *Is* the New Sales

We're living in the era where traditional sales tactics are dying, and influence is taking over. By 2024, the surge of influencer marketing pushed social media ahead of paid search to become the world's leading advertising platform, generating $247.3 billion in global investment. Spending is expected to climb to $266.9 billion by the end of 2025, underscoring influencers' central role in shaping consumer behavior and engagement.*

However, here's something I don't want people in the relationship business to miss: The principles that make great influencers successful are the same principles that make great salespeople successful.

The difference is traditional salespeople were taught to influence people in a thirty-minute meeting or phone call. Today's most successful "influencers" understand they're building influence over months and years through consistent, valuable content and authentic relationship building.

But there's a crucial distinction between manufactured influence and authentic influence. Manufactured influence relies on follower counts, viral content, and paid partnerships. Authentic influence is built on trust, consistency, and genuine care for the people you serve.

The salespeople thriving in this new era aren't the ones with the slickest presentations; they're the ones who've become trusted advisors in their space. They share valuable insights regularly. They educate before they sell. They build relationships before they ask for anything.

In other words, they've figured out how to be "influencers" in their industry, even if they never call themselves that. They understand that in a world where everyone has access to information, trust becomes the ultimate currency.

The most successful salespeople I know aren't the ones with the best closing techniques or the most aggressive approaches. They're the ones who have mastered the art of building genuine relationships. They're the ones who understand that trust is the ultimate currency in business.

---

* Influencer Marketing Hub, "Influencer Marketing Benchmark Report 2025," April 25, 2025, https://influencermarketinghub.com/influencer-marketing-benchmark-report/.

They're the ones who know that a relationship built on trust is worth more than a hundred transactions built on pressure.

Before you close this chapter thinking, *This all sounds nice, but it won't work for me*, let me address the three objections I hear most often.

"This sounds nice, but I work in [industry], where relationships don't matter."

I've heard this from software salespeople, pharmaceutical reps, car salesmen, insurance agents, and even social media marketers. Here's the thing: There is *no* industry where relationships don't matter.

The more commoditized your product or service, the more relationships matter. When everyone is selling essentially the same thing at roughly the same price, the relationship becomes the differentiator. Even in highly technical B2B sales where decisions seem purely logical, people still buy from people they trust.

Think about it: When was the last time you bought something significant from someone you didn't like or trust? Even when you're buying the cheapest option online, you're still looking at reviews—you're still seeking some form of social proof that other people had a good relationship with this seller.

"I don't have time to build relationships—I need results now."

This is the scarcity mindset talking. Here's the paradox: The people who say they don't have time to build relationships are usually the ones working the hardest for the least results.

Building relationships doesn't take more time—it takes *different* time. Instead of spending hours cold-calling strangers who don't trust you, you spend minutes nurturing relationships with people who already do. Instead of chasing hundreds of leads, you focus on dozens of quality relationships.

The fastest way to get results is to stop chasing quick wins and start building something sustainable. A single referral from a trusted relationship can be worth more than a hundred cold calls.

"My company only cares about numbers, not relationships."

Here's a secret: Companies that claim to only care about numbers are usually the ones struggling to hit their numbers. The smartest companies understand that relationships drive numbers.

But even if your company is purely numbers-focused, you can still build relationships within that framework. Hit your numbers by building relationships, not despite them. Track your relationship metrics alongside your sales metrics. Show how your referral rate correlates with your closing rate. Demonstrate that your relationship-focused approach is actually driving better numbers.

The companies that survive and thrive long-term are the ones that understand that behind every number is a person, and behind every person is a potential relationship.

The Cautionary Tale: What Happens When Relationships Don't Matter

Let me tell you about Jake (not his real name), a fellow agent in my office who was the poster child for transactional selling. Jake was aggressive, fast-talking, and incredibly skilled at closing deals. He had memorized every objection handler in the book and could overcome any resistance. For two years, Jake consistently outsold everyone in our office.

Jake would brag about his "hit it and quit it" approach. He'd close a deal, collect his commission, and move on to the next prospect. He never followed up after closing unless there was a problem. He never sent birthday cards or holiday greetings. He never asked about his clients' families or remembered personal details. "I'm not their friend," he'd say. "I'm their real estate agent."

And it worked—until it didn't.

In year three, Jake's business began to slow. He wasn't getting repeat clients because his previous clients didn't really know him. He wasn't getting referrals because his clients didn't trust him enough to risk their reputation by recommending him. When the market shifted and new leads became scarce, Jake had nothing to fall back on.

Meanwhile, agents like me—who had been focused on relationships—were thriving. Our past clients were coming back, referring friends, and staying loyal even when competitors offered lower prices. We had built businesses that were recession-proof because they were built on relationships.

Jake eventually left real estate. His aggressive tactics that had brought short-term success became his long-term downfall. He had mastered the art of closing deals but had never learned the art of building relationships.

The moral of the story: You can push, pressure, and manipulate your way to short-term success, but you can't build a sustainable business without authentic relationships.

The Universal Truth: It Works Everywhere

You might be thinking, *But Barb, you built your sales career in real estate. That's different from my industry.*

Here's what *Harvard Business Review* discovered: Eighty-four percent of B2B decision-makers start their buying process with a referral, not a cold call.* Think about that for a moment. The vast majority of business decisions begin with someone saying, "I know someone who can help you with that."

B2B Software Sales: What if you actually used your prospect's current software for a week and documented the specific pain points? What if you sent a three-minute video walking through exactly how you'd solve their top workflow bottleneck before they even agree to a demo? The response rates speak for themselves.

Retail Automotive: What if you texted customers a photo when you spotted their exact car model during your commute, just to say, "Saw your twin on I-95 today—hope you're loving yours!"? What if you remembered they mentioned their daughter was learning to drive and checked in when she got her license? When their friends needed cars, whose name would come up at barbecues?

Insurance Sales: What if you were the agent who showed up with coffee when clients were dealing with a claim—not to sell anything, just to help navigate the paperwork? What if you sent birthday cards to their kids, not marketing materials? When policy renewal time came, would price even be a consideration if the relationship was valuable enough?

Professional Services/Consulting: What if you're selling consulting services, and instead of just meeting with C-suite executives, you grab

---

* Laurence Minsky and Keith A. Quesenberry, "How B2B Sales Can Benefit from Social Selling," *Harvard Business Review*, November 8, 2016, https://hbr.org/2016/11/84-of-b2b-sales-start-with-a-referral-not-a-salesperson.

coffee with the department heads who actually have to implement your recommendations? What if you learned their names, understood their team dynamics, and showed genuine interest in making their jobs easier—not just impressing their bosses? When decision time came, who do you think those department heads would advocate for in the boardroom?

Commercial Real Estate: What if you're leasing office space, and instead of just talking square footage with facilities managers, you chatted with the actual employees about their commute, their lunch spots, and their parking frustrations? What if you understood what would make their daily work life better? When the lease decision came down to two similar properties, which broker do you think they'd recommend to their boss?

Financial Services/Banking: What if you're selling business loans and instead of just running credit reports, you spend time understanding the business owner's daily cash flow challenges? What if you knew their busy seasons, their supplier relationships, and their growth dreams? When they needed financing, would they shop around or call you first?

Marketing Agency Services: What if instead of just pitching campaign ideas to marketing directors, you took time to understand the sales team's lead quality complaints? What if you learned what keeps the CEO up at night about customer acquisition? When budget season came, who would they fight to keep in the room?

Pharmaceutical Sales: What if instead of just pushing products, you brought research relevant to physicians' specific patient populations? What if you remembered details about their practice challenges and became a trusted resource rather than just another sales rep?

There's a common thread here. In every case, the salesperson who focuses on relationships outperforms those who focus on transactions. The industry doesn't matter. The product doesn't matter. The relationship matters.

When applying relationship ranking to sales, I always tell salespeople to rank their relationships based on two factors: the level of relationship combined with their ability to refer you.

My best friend Katrina is an elementary school teacher. In my personal life, she's a five-star relationship. In my real estate sales career, she is also a five-star relationship because she is super close to me, a strong advocate, and has the ability to refer me to other teachers, parents, and community members. But in my speaking business, she's not a five-star relationship—not because I love her any less, but because she doesn't have a high ability to refer me for corporate speaking engagements. The ranking isn't about the person's worth; it's about strategic resource allocation.

This applies across every industry. That pharmaceutical rep needs to identify which physicians not only trust them but also influence other doctors' prescribing decisions. The software salesperson should focus on clients who are not just satisfied but also well-connected in industry associations or online communities. The insurance agent's five-star relationships aren't just happy clients—they're the ones who naturally talk about insurance at neighborhood gatherings and business networking events.

The relationship-first approach works everywhere, but the Relationship Operating System ensures you're building those relationships strategically, and investing your time where it will generate the highest return in referrals and repeat business.

The "What If" Vision: Your Business Transformed

Stop for a moment and imagine this scenario:

What if every client became a referral source? Picture walking into work tomorrow knowing that you don't have to make cold calls because your phone is ringing with warm referrals. Imagine having prospects call you saying, "My friend Susan said you're the only person I should talk to about this."

Envision having a business where:

- Your closing rate is 80 percent because people are referred to you by someone they trust.
- Your average sale size is higher because trust eliminates price objections.
- Your sales cycle is shorter because you're starting with established credibility.
- Your work is more fulfilling because you're solving problems for people who already want to work with you.
- Your income is predictable because it's built on relationships, not random prospecting.

What if your biggest challenge wasn't finding new clients but managing the referrals you already have?

This isn't fantasy; this is the reality for salespeople who have mastered the relationship advantage. When you build genuine relationships, every satisfied client becomes a sales team member. Every successful interaction becomes a marketing campaign. Every problem you solve becomes a case study that attracts more ideal clients. This is what happened to me!

What if you could build a business that runs itself?

When relationships are your foundation, your business becomes self-sustaining. Past clients return for additional services. Referrals flow naturally. Your reputation precedes you. You're not selling anymore; you're consulting with people who already trust you.

The most successful salespeople I know spend less time selling and more time serving because they've built a relationship-driven business that attracts the right clients naturally.

What if Monday mornings felt different? Instead of dreading another week of cold calls and rejections, you'd wake up excited to connect with people who value your expertise. Instead of worrying about hitting quotas, you'd focus on serving clients who see you as a trusted advisor.

This is the power of the relationship advantage. This is what's possible when you stop chasing transactions and start building connections. The question isn't whether this vision is possible—it's whether you're willing to do what it takes to make it your reality.

Relationship Building at Scale

There's a fundamental truth that most ambitious people learn too late: You can't scale success if you don't scale your relationships.

Every entrepreneur, leader, and high achiever eventually hits the same wall. They've maxed out their personal capacity—they're working longer hours, optimizing every process, leveraging every skill they have—but their growth has plateaued. They're trapped in the myth that success is a solo sport.

Here's what they miss: Success isn't limited by your personal capacity; it's limited by your *relational capacity*. Your ability to grow beyond where you are today depends entirely on your ability to build relationships with people who can open doors you can't reach, solve problems you can't solve, and create opportunities you can't create alone.

Think about it mathematically. As a solopreneur, your success is capped by the number of hours you can work and the value you can personally deliver. But when you build authentic relationships, you multiply your capacity exponentially. Every genuine connection becomes a potential collaborator, referral source, advisor, or advocate.

One relationship can ten-times your business overnight. The right introduction can open a market you've been trying to crack for years. A single referral from someone who trusts you can be worth more than months of cold outreach. But these multiplier effects only happen when you've invested genuinely in relationships before you need them.

The entrepreneurs who scale successfully understand this instinctively. They don't just build products or services—they build ecosystems of relationships. They don't just focus on customer acquisition—they focus on creating advocates who become their unpaid sales force. They don't just network—they systematically invest in people who can accelerate their growth.

But here's the catch: You can't fake this. You can't build relationships only when you need to scale. Authentic relationships take time to develop, trust to establish, and value to accumulate. The relationships that will scale your success tomorrow are the ones you're building today.

That truth leads to one of the most common objections I hear: "Barb, this all sounds great for building deep relationships with a few dozen people, but what about businesses with hundreds or thousands of customers? How do you scale authentic relationship building?"

The answer is simple: The principles don't change, but the systems do. Whether you're serving fifty clients or five thousand customers, the goal remains the same: Make people feel seen, known, and important. The difference is in how you systematize that care.

Let me share three stories that perfectly illustrate relationship building at scale, from a small independent restaurant, a luxury hotel chain, an online retailer, and the world's biggest touring artist.

The Spaghettini Story: When Systems Remember What Matters

Spaghettini is an independent Italian restaurant in Seal Beach, California—the kind of place where regulars feel like family and first-time visitors leave planning their return. I knew Terri, one of their servers, before I ever started going to the restaurant. Our kids played baseball together, so when I decided to try Spaghettini, I was excited to see a familiar face.

Terri has been there for over thirty years, since the restaurant opened, and her relationship-building and customer-service skills are off the charts. She remembers not just your usual order but also your kids' names and the details that make you feel known.

Early in my gluten-free journey, I mentioned my dietary restrictions to Terri during one of my visits. She was incredibly attentive, making sure I had options. Over the next few visits, she began surprising me by bringing out gluten-free bread without me even asking. I was touched by her thoughtfulness and assumed this was just Terri being the exceptional person I knew her to be.

But then came the night that changed everything.

I made a reservation for a Friday evening, and when I arrived, Terri wasn't working. We were seated with a different server, someone I'd never met before. When the breadbasket came to the table, I noticed it included gluten-free bread alongside the regular bread. I was shocked.

"How'd you know I needed gluten-free options?" I asked the server. "Is Terri here tonight?"

"No, Terri's not working," she replied with a smile. "But it's in your customer record. We have a note that you require gluten-free bread."

I was stunned. What I thought was one person's exceptional memory was actually a restaurant's systematic approach to relationship building. Terri had taken the time to enter my dietary needs into their customer management system, ensuring that every time I came in, regardless of who was serving me, my preferences would be known and honored.

This small gesture—anticipating my needs before I even have to ask—has created incredible loyalty. I don't just return to Spaghettini because the food is good. (It is.) I return because they've shown me that my preferences matter enough to remember and act on them consistently, regardless of which team member is serving me.

That's the power of scaling relationship building—using systems to ensure that every customer feels the care that exceptional employees like Terri naturally provide.

The Joshie Story: When Companies Create Memories, Not Just Solutions

The Ritz-Carlton Hotel Company has built their entire brand around relationship building at scale, but one story perfectly illustrates how their systems enable extraordinary individual care.

A family was staying at the Ritz-Carlton, Amelia Island, when their young son lost his beloved stuffed giraffe somewhere in the hotel. The child was inconsolable, and despite the staff's best efforts, they couldn't locate the toy. The family had to leave for their flight home with a heartbroken little boy.

The Ritz-Carlton could have simply found Joshie and mailed him back in a box. That would have been good customer service. Instead, they chose to create a memory.

The staff "found" Joshie the Giraffe and created an elaborate story about his extended vacation at the resort. They took photos of Joshie lounging by the pool, getting a massage at the spa, and enjoying room service. They created a photo album documenting Joshie's "vacation" and even included an official Ritz-Carlton employee ID card showing that Joshie was now part of the team. They mailed the entire package to the family along with the stuffed animal.

The child was delighted, the parents were amazed, and the story went viral, generating millions of dollars' worth of positive publicity for the Ritz-Carlton. But more importantly, they created customers for life and demonstrated that relationship building at scale doesn't mean losing the personal touch—it means systematizing the ability to create exceptional moments that become cherished memories.

This single act created a ripple effect across the Ritz-Carlton's entire network. When this story spread, it didn't just elevate the Amelia Island location; it reinforced the brand promise at every Ritz-Carlton property nationwide.

This is the power of systematic relationship building. When you create a process that enables extraordinary individual care, each exceptional moment doesn't just impact that one relationship; it elevates your entire brand and creates expectations that drive business to every part of your organization.

The Chewy Story: When Compassion Becomes Company Policy

Chewy, an online pet supply retailer, has built their business around understanding that pets aren't just animals—they're family members. This understanding shows up most powerfully in how they handle one of the most difficult moments pet owners face: loss.

When customers call to return unopened pet food because their beloved pet has passed away, most companies would process a standard return and refund. Chewy's customer service representatives are empowered to do something extraordinary: They refund the customer's money, tell them to donate the food to a local animal shelter instead of returning it, and often send a personalized sympathy gift—sometimes a hand-painted portrait of the customer's pet or flowers with a heartfelt condolence note.

These gestures aren't random acts of kindness—they're built into Chewy's operating procedures. The company has systematized compassion, empowering their team to turn moments of grief into expressions of genuine care. The result? Customers who are going through one of the most difficult experiences of pet ownership remember Chewy not just as a vendor but as a company that truly understood their loss.

The Taylor Swift Story: When Authenticity Scales to Stadiums

Taylor Swift didn't become the highest-grossing touring artist in history by accident. She built a billion-dollar empire on something far more powerful than marketing: authentic relationships, built one person at a time.

In her early career, Swift did something established artists rarely do—she stayed after every concert to meet fans personally. Not quick photo ops, but real conversations. She would spend hours talking with fans about their lives, remembering details from previous encounters, and making each person feel genuinely seen.

She's known for writing handwritten notes to fans going through difficult times—not generic messages, but personal letters that reference specific details from their conversations. She sends flowers to celebrate their milestones. She bakes them cookies for the holidays. These weren't calculated marketing moves; they were systematic expressions of genuine care that built her fan base one relationship at a time.

While other artists focused on reaching the masses, Swift focused on connecting with individuals. She understood that one meaningful conversation could create a fan for life—and that fan would naturally share their experience. The result? Exponential returns. Fans who felt personally valued became passionate advocates, convincing entire social networks to attend concerts and buy albums.

Her Eras Tour became the highest-grossing tour in history, with fans traveling across continents and spending thousands of dollars for the experience. But they're not just buying tickets—they're investing in a relationship that feels personal and meaningful.

Swift proved that when you invest genuinely in individuals, they don't just become customers—they become advocates who create movements around what you're building. The same principle applies in business: massive success isn't built through mass marketing—it's built one authentic relationship at a time.

The Principles That Scale

All four of these stories illustrate the same core principles that make relationship building scalable:

Systems That Capture What Matters: Whether it's a restaurant's reservation system noting dietary preferences, a hotel's guest service software tracking special requests, a pet retailer's customer service protocols for loss, or an artist's personal notes and gestures, the key is capturing and acting on the details that matter to customers.

Empowered Employees: Terri didn't need management approval to enter my preferences in the system. The Ritz-Carlton staff didn't need permission to create Joshie's vacation album. Chewy representatives don't need approval to send sympathy gifts. And Taylor Swift built her own personal system for follow-up and recognition. Companies that scale relationship building empower their employees to act on customer needs immediately.

Consistent Experience Regardless of Touchpoint: At Spaghettini, any server can provide my gluten-free bread because the system supports it. At the Ritz-Carlton, any employee can access guest preferences and create exceptional experiences. At Chewy, any customer service representative can respond with compassion because it's built into their training and procedures. At Taylor Swift concerts, fans everywhere feel personally connected—because her approach is consistent and sincere.

Surprise and Delight Becomes Standard: All four of these stories have systematized going beyond expectations. It's not an accident or a one-time gesture—it's how they operate consistently.

Creating Your Scalable Relationship System

Here's how to apply these principles regardless of your business size:

Document What Matters: Create systems to capture customer preferences, important dates, family information, and interaction history. Whether it's a simple spreadsheet or sophisticated customer relationship management (CRM) system, the tool doesn't matter. The intention does.

Train for Relationship Building: Your team needs to understand that every interaction is an opportunity to strengthen the relationship. This isn't just customer service; it's relationship maintenance at scale.

Empower Action: Give your team the authority and resources to solve problems and create exceptional moments without requiring approval for every decision.

Make Preferences Portable: Ensure that customer information and preferences are accessible to anyone who might serve them so the quality of care doesn't depend on which team member they encounter.

Systematize Surprise: Build unexpected touches into your standard processes. Maybe it's remembering birthdays, sending follow-up notes, or going beyond what's expected—but make these gestures part of your systematic approach, not random acts of kindness.

The Compound Effect of Systematic Care

When you scale relationship building effectively, something powerful happens—customers become advocates. They don't just return—they bring others. They don't just buy—they refer. They don't just appreciate good service—they become emotional ambassadors for your brand.

The key insight is that relationship building at scale isn't about mass personalization or complex technology. It's about systematizing care so that every customer feels the attention and intentionality that exceptional individuals naturally provide. The systems may get more sophisticated, but the heart of relationship building remains beautifully simple—pay attention to what matters to people, remember it, and act on it consistently.

Because in the end, customers don't want to feel like numbers in your database. They want to feel like Terri knows their dietary needs, Joshie gets to have an adventure, and Chewy understands that losing a pet is losing a family member. When you can deliver that feeling systematically, you've mastered relationship building at scale.

Your Sales Relationship Shift Starts Now

With the right mindset, tools, and focus on relationships, you'll find that the true power of sales lies in the connections you build and the trust you earn. Remember: Whether you're convincing your toddler to tie their shoes or closing a million-dollar deal, it's all about relationships. It's all about trust. It's all about showing up as your authentic self and genuinely caring about the people you're trying to serve.

Stop chasing transactions. Start building relationships. Your future self—and your bank account—will thank you.

Because in the end, we're all in sales. The question is, are you selling transactions, or are you building relationships that last?

The choice is yours. Make it count.

CHAPTER 12

Leadership Through Connection: When Trust Becomes Your Greatest Currency

Most people think leadership is about having the right answers, making the tough decisions, and driving results. But what if I told you that the most powerful leaders are those who make people feel like they belong? That the secret to building unstoppable teams isn't found in strategy sessions, key performance indicators (KPIs), or performance metrics, but in creating a place where people feel genuinely seen, valued, and connected?

I learned this truth by building my entire real estate company one relationship at a time. No recruiting, no cold-calling, no begging agents to join me. Just authentic connection. And I learned it again, more painfully, when I nearly lost everything by forgetting what had built it all in the first place.

Creating a Home Where People Belong

When I started my company, I had no choice but to build through relationships. I was an "indie" broker (aka independent broker). I didn't have a big name, a fancy office, or deep pockets to attract talent. What I had was time, genuine interest in people, and an unwavering belief that the right relationships could build anything.

But this wasn't just about business strategy; it was about creating something deeper. I wanted to build the kind of place I'd always wanted to be a part of. Somewhere I felt known and with a fantastic culture. Somewhere where my contributions mattered and where I could grow without fear of being left behind.

In those early days, I spent hours in coffee shops and networking events, not looking for recruits but looking for connections. I'd ask questions like, "What's working in your business?" and "What's your biggest challenge right now?" Instead of pitching my opportunity, I'd listen. Really listen. Then I'd follow up with resources, introductions, or simple encouragement.

The agents who eventually joined my team didn't come because I convinced them. They came because they already felt known and valued. By the time they were ready to make a move, joining my company felt like coming home rather than changing brokerages.

This approach created something magical. Our morning meetings weren't just about numbers and goals; they were about connection. We checked in on each other's lives. We celebrated personal wins alongside professional ones. We created space for vulnerability, for questions, for growth. I knew the anxiety in one team member's voice when her daughter started preschool for the first time, and I made sure to text her that afternoon to see how drop-off went. When one of our agent's elderly father was hospitalized, we all rallied around her, covering her showings and client calls without being asked. When another team member's baby was born prematurely and spent weeks in the NICU, I was the first person outside of the family to come hold her tiny daughter, because that's what family does for each other.

All these moments weren't just office small talk; they were the foundation of everything we built together. These moments of genuine care created bonds that went far beyond professional relationships. We became a family, and our office felt like home.

When someone was struggling, we rallied around them. When someone succeeded, we celebrated together. When someone needed to grow, we invested in their development even when it meant they might outgrow us. This is what relational leadership looks like: putting people first, knowing that results follow relationships.

Our company became known not just for our results but for our culture. Other agents wanted to join us. We'd created more than just another real estate brokerage; we'd created a home where people belonged.

The Story I Don't Want to Tell

Here's the part that's hardest to write but perhaps most important to share. I'm the relationship expert. I speak on stages about the power of human connection. I'm writing an entire book on it. Yet I still got it catastrophically wrong. This is the story of how I built everything through relationships and nearly lost it all by forgetting what had built it in the first place.

The foundation was solid. Over the years, I had carefully assembled a team of extraordinary women and a few remarkable men. Each person had been chosen not just for their skills but for who they were as human beings. We had systems, structure, and support. But more than that, we had a connection. I was the leader people could count on, emotionally present, deeply involved, and genuinely invested in each person's success and happiness.

Supporting me through it all was my assistant—a woman who had become my right and left hand. She knew the business inside and out, understood our culture, and shared my commitment to putting relationships first. I trusted her completely, and that trust felt like one of my greatest leadership successes.

Then the speaking opportunities began to grow. What started as local real estate events expanded to women's conferences, leadership summits, and corporate events. Each invitation felt like validation of the message I'd been living—that relationships were the key to everything. Standing on those stages, sharing my story, and inspiring others to build through connection filled me with a purpose I'd never experienced before.

As the speaking career gained momentum, I found myself pulled in two directions. There was the real estate company that had given me everything, and there was this new world of possibility that seemed to be calling my name. I convinced myself I could do both. After all, hadn't I built everything on strong relationships? Surely those bonds were deep enough to weather my divided attention.

Slowly, almost imperceptibly, I began to shift responsibilities to my assistant. At first, it was just more of the administrative tasks. But gradually, as speaking engagements took me away from the office more frequently, she began handling more of the day-to-day interactions with my agents.

I told myself this was a smart delegation. I was developing her leadership skills while building my speaking platform. The systems we'd created were strong enough to run themselves, and my assistant was more than capable of handling the day-to-day operations while I was away.

But one thing I was reminded of was that relationships can't be delegated. Connection can't be outsourced. Trust can't be transferred from one person to another like a file folder.

What I didn't realize was that with each speaking engagement—with each day I spent focused on building my personal brand rather than maintaining our team culture—the gravitational center of our company was shifting. What I didn't know was happening was that the relationships were strengthening with her and weakening with me. My assistant wasn't just handling my responsibilities; she was becoming the person our team members turned to for support, guidance, and connection. The relationships that had once centered around me began to orbit around her instead.

The first crack appeared when my top agent, Danielle, someone I had personally mentored from assistant to six-figure earner, came into my office and said, "We need to talk." She stepped in and closed the door. She had been with me for eight years. I'd taught her everything I knew about the business, about client relationships, and about building a career in real estate. She was like family. And she was darn good at real estate.

"I've learned so much from you," she said, her voice careful and measured. "But I've outgrown this. I want to start my own team, and I can't do that here with you."

Her words hit me like a physical blow. *Outgrown me? How is that possible?* I was still her leader, still invested in her success. But as she talked, I realized that while I'd been focused on building my speaking career, she had been building her own vision, one that no longer included me. The mentorship that had once been so central to our relationship had become sporadic and surface-level.

Then came the domino effect. Within a month, two more top producers followed, some joining her new team, others finding their own paths. The reasons were always professional and diplomatic, but the message was clear: They were following the relationships that felt most real, most present, and most connected. And those relationships were no longer with me.

But it was the call from one of my favorite agents, Beth, a really dear friend, that hit me the hardest. When she told me she was leaving, I was sad and heartbroken. When I asked her why, she said something I will never forget: "You've forgotten about me. I haven't closed a deal in six months, and you haven't even checked in on me just to see how I'm doing or offer help."

Her words hit me like a ton of bricks. She was right. It's not that I had forgotten about her, but I did take her for granted. This woman had been not just an agent but a friend. I had been so focused on my speaking career that I hadn't noticed her struggling. The leader who used to check in on preschool drop-offs and hospital visits had missed six months of professional and personal struggle.

My assistant's departure came later, but it felt like the final blow. After being by my side for eleven years, she had found an opportunity at another company that offered her more growth potential. In our final conversation, she thanked me for everything I'd taught her about relationships and leadership. The irony was devastating. I had taught her so well that she had become indispensable to our team, but I had been too absent to remain indispensable to her.

In less than six months, more than half my team was gone. They hadn't left because of money or even dissatisfaction with our company. They had followed the connection, just as I had always taught them to do. Many agents left because they felt more connected to my assistant than to me. I had made my assistant the center of their world, completely by accident. The problem was that the connection was no longer with me.

Sitting in my half-empty office, surrounded by vacant desks that had once buzzed with energy and laughter, I had to face the most painful truth of my career: I had violated every principle I taught. The woman who built everything through relationships had let those relationships wither through neglect. The leader who preached the importance of connection had become disconnected from the very people who mattered most.

The home I had worked so hard to create for others no longer felt like home because I hadn't been there to maintain it.

When you're not intentionally building human connection, you're unintentionally losing it.

I could have blamed my agents and my assistant for "stealing" my team. I could have blamed the team members for being disloyal. But the truth was simpler and more painful: I had failed as a relational leader. The woman who spoke on stages about the power of connection had stopped connecting. The leader who built everything through relationships had let those relationships atrophy.

So I had to do the hardest thing a leader can do: I had to admit it. I came to the loyal ones who stayed and had the most difficult conversation of my career. I told them the truth. I acknowledged that I'd lost focus on what mattered most. I admitted that I'd taken our relationships for granted. I explained that I'd tried to build something new without maintaining what I'd already built, and that the failure was entirely mine.

Then I made a commitment. I couldn't promise I wouldn't pursue other opportunities, but I could promise that I would never again let our relationships drift away. I would be present, engaged, and intentional about the connections that made everything else possible.

This wasn't just about rebuilding a team; it was about rebuilding the home we'd created together. And home requires someone to be present, to maintain it, to make it a place people want to return to every day.

What Relational Leadership Really Means

The experience taught me that relational leadership isn't just about being nice or building rapport. It's about understanding that you're not just managing a team; you're creating, protecting, and maintaining a space where people can belong, grow, and thrive.

Relational leaders understand that authority might get you compliance, but relationships get you commitment.

They know that people don't leave companies; they leave leaders. More importantly, they know that people don't just join companies; they join cultures created by leaders who see them as whole human beings, not just producers.

Relational leaders prioritize humans over numbers. They understand that when you take care of the people, the people take care of the business. They invest in personal growth, celebrate individual wins, and create space for vulnerability and authenticity.

Relational leaders make people feel seen and known. They remember personal details, check in during tough times, and show up for the moments that matter. They understand that leadership happens in the spaces between meetings, in the quick conversations, and in the follow-up texts.

Relational leaders create belonging, not just employment. They build cultures where people feel safe to be themselves, where they can grow without fear, and where they're valued for who they are, not just what they produce.

Relational leaders are multipliers. They don't just build their own networks; they help others build theirs. They don't just create their own opportunities; they create opportunities for others. They understand that their success is measured not by what they achieve alone, but by what they make possible for others.

Most importantly, relational leaders understand that this isn't a strategy you can implement and then move on from; it's a daily commitment that requires constant attention and intention.

How to Prevent Relationship Drift: Lessons from My Failure

My story isn't unique. Every day, leaders lose great people not because of money or opportunities, but because relationships drift away through neglect. The good news is that relationship drift is preventable . . . if you're intentional about it.

Here's what I wish I had known then and what I practice now.

Create Non-Delegable Relationship Rituals

Not everything can be delegated, and relationships top that list. Identify the connection points that only you can and should handle:

Personal check-ins that only you do. These aren't performance reviews or business updates. They're conversations about life, challenges, dreams, and how someone is really doing. Schedule them frequently and guard them fiercely.

Victory celebrations that come from you personally. When someone wins, they should hear from you first. A text, a call, a personal note, or something that says their success matters to you personally, not just professionally.

Presence during difficult times. When someone is struggling personally or professionally, they need to hear from the leader, not the assistant. Show up for hospital visits, family emergencies, and career crossroads.

Monitor Your Connection Temperature

Most leaders track sales numbers, productivity metrics, and financial performance religiously. But how many track relationship health? Start asking yourself these questions weekly:

When was the last time I had a meaningful conversation with each team member? If you can't remember, it's been too long. Meaningful means beyond work tasks—it means knowing what's happening in their world.

Are my conversations becoming purely transactional? If you're only talking about deals, deadlines, and deliverables, you're moving into dangerous territory. Relationships require personal connection, not just professional interaction.

Who am I losing touch with? Pay special attention to your high performers and your quiet contributors. High performers often get less attention because they seem fine, and quiet people can disappear entirely if you're not intentional.

Build Systems That Support Presence, Not Replace It

Technology and systems should enhance your relationship building, never replace it.

Use reminders for personal details, but deliver the care personally. Keep notes about family situations, hobbies, and important dates, but the follow-up should always come from you directly.

Create accountability for your own relationship maintenance. Put relationship check-ins on your calendar like any other important meeting. Block time for relationship building and protect it as fiercely as you would a client meeting.

Stay Present in the Small Moments

Leadership happens in the spaces between the big moments. It's built in hallway conversations, quick texts, and remembered details.

Be physically present when you say you will be. If you promise to be at the morning meeting, be there. If you say you'll stop by someone's desk, do it. Reliability in small things builds trust for big things.

Remember and follow up on personal milestones. First days of school, medical appointments, family visits, and vacation plans matter to people, so they should matter to you. Set reminders and actually use them.

Notice changes in behavior or energy. When someone who's usually upbeat seems off, when a high performer starts struggling, or when someone becomes quieter than usual, these are signals that require your attention, not delegation to someone else.

Have the Honest Conversations Early

Don't wait for exit interviews to discover relationship problems. Create space for honest feedback about your leadership and presence.

Ask directly about connection. In your one-on-ones, ask questions like, "How connected do you feel to me and the team?" and "What do you need from me that you're not getting?"

Address relationship drift before it becomes departure. If you sense distance growing, name it. Say something like, "I feel like we've become more distant lately, and I want to understand what's happening."

Make space for feedback about your leadership presence. Ask your team members to tell you when you're becoming too absent or too focused on other priorities. Give them permission to call you out when relationships start to drift.

Learn to Recognize the Warning Signs

Relationship drift doesn't happen overnight—it's a gradual process with clear warning signs.

Conversations become shorter and more surface-level. When deep connections start turning into quick updates, pay attention.

People stop coming to you with problems. If team members start going to others with issues they used to bring to you, that's a red flag.

Personal sharing decreases. When people stop telling you about their lives outside of work, the relationship is moving in the wrong direction.

You start hearing important news secondhand. If you're learning about major developments in your team members' lives from other people, you've lost connection.

The truth is, preventing relationship drift requires the same intentionality that building relationships does in the first place. It's not enough to build strong connections; you have to maintain them with the same energy and attention you used to create them.

My failure taught me that relationships are like plants; they require consistent care to thrive. You can't water them once and expect them to survive on their own. But when you tend to them daily, when you show up consistently, when you prioritize connection over convenience, you create something that can weather any storm.

Don't learn this lesson the way I did. Don't wait until half your team is gone to realize that relationships can't be delegated. Start today. Check in on someone. Ask about their life, not just their work. Show up when it matters. Because in the end, your success as a leader isn't measured by what you build; it's measured by who stays to build it with you.

The Ongoing Practice

Leadership through connection isn't a destination; it's a daily practice. It's choosing to invest in relationships even when you're busy—especially when you're busy. It's remembering that people don't just work for companies; they work for leaders who see them, value them, and invest in their growth.

It's understanding that trust is both the foundation and the goal of all meaningful leadership. Without trust, you have compliance at best. With trust, you have commitment, creativity, and the kind of culture that attracts the best people and inspires them to do their best work.

The cost of getting this wrong is higher than most leaders realize. It's not just about turnover or performance metrics; it's about the human cost of broken trust and missed opportunities to make a real difference in people's lives.

The reward for getting it right is everything: teams that thrive, cultures that attract top talent, leaders who create other leaders, and the deep satisfaction of knowing you've built something meaningful through the power of genuine human connection.

When you lead through relationships, you create more than a successful business; you create a home where people belong. And in a world that's increasingly disconnected, that sense of belonging becomes your greatest competitive advantage.

Because at the end of the day, people will forget what you said and what you did, but they'll never forget how you made them feel. And if you can make them feel like they belong, like they matter, like they're part of something bigger than themselves, you'll have their loyalty, their commitment, and their best work for life.

That's the power of leadership through connection. That's what happens when relationships become your strategy.

CHAPTER 13

Building Communities, Not Just Networks

I've lost count of how many times I've walked into an event or a ballroom and saw someone with my exact credentials—similar years in real estate, comparable sales numbers, even the same coaching program on their résumé. On paper, we looked identical. We'd paid the same registration fees, sat through the same sessions, and had access to the same networking opportunities. But we'd built our businesses completely differently.

While some worked the room collecting business cards and pitching their services to anyone who would listen, I focused on real conversations. I remember one Buffini & Company event where an agent methodically moved through the room, spending three minutes with each person before moving on to the next "opportunity." Meanwhile, I spent the entire break with one struggling agent from Arizona, learning about her market challenges and brainstorming solutions. She never sent me a single referral—but she introduced me to her mentor, who became one of my most valuable professional relationships.

The difference wasn't our backgrounds or our business knowledge. The difference was how we showed up. Over seventeen years in that community, I watched countless agents with impressive credentials come and go, while others built thriving networks that sustained them through market shifts and industry changes. The distinction was never about what they knew—it was about the relationships they chose to nurture.

There's something magical that happens when you put yourself in a room full of people who share your ambitions, your challenges, and your commitment to growth. It's not just networking; it's community building. And the difference between the two has shaped every major breakthrough in my career.

Communities aren't just about shared interests; they're about shared journeys. When you surround yourself with like-minded people, people with a shared interest in something, or people on the same journey as you, you create an environment where growth accelerates, opportunities multiply, and relationships deepen in ways that transform both your business and your life.

But here's what I've learned: Simply being in the room isn't enough. How you show up in that room determines whether you'll build a network that transforms your business or just collect a stack of business cards that gather dust.

The Long-Term Impact of Authentic Community

After seventeen years of membership, I'm no longer part of that organization, but I literally still "do life" with these people. I know their families. I've visited their homes. I've done business with them. What started as a professional coaching relationship evolved into genuine friendships that have outlasted the formal membership and continue to enrich both my business and my personal life.

Like Todd Nordstrom, my dear friend and brother from South Beach, Miami. Todd is the funniest person I know, someone who can lighten any conversation with his humor and infectious laughter. He's also a Disney drama queen (literally), and I mean, who else visits Disney multiple times a year by themselves? But beyond the laughs, Todd has been there for me and countless others in practical ways. When my clients or friends need help in South Beach, Miami, Todd is my go-to person. He's proven over and over that these community relationships create real value in real ways. And Dan and Maria O'Dell, who were huge mentors of ours in our real estate business—not to mention they've always shown great love and affection for our children—and most recently have helped us pivot and reorganize our company when we needed it the most. They were there with the exact tools and resources we needed. A visit with them is always on the top of our list when we visit Kansas City.

Or Mike Lopez and Eric Johnson. I met both of them at Buffini & Company when they were in leadership roles within the company. We developed genuine relationships and friendships over the years. For various reasons, they both eventually left the company. Fast-forward to my own exit—I knew I needed to still have a coach and accountability partner, someone to see my blind spots. Who better than two of the key people who understood how I worked, what I valued, and what I might miss by leaving the community? They had started their own consulting company, and my husband and I signed up and have been with them ever since. They helped us build our real estate team and transition to a brokerage and still help us today, including with my speaking career. All because of that shared connection and passion we built years ago in that original community.

And then there's Heather Valentine. We met at a cocktail reception at an elite conference where we were easily the youngest people in the room. I remember thinking, *I'm supposed to be the youngest person here*, and wondering, *How do I not know her?* We were sizing each other up from across the space until someone we now call Mom—Mary Beth Eisenhard, who nurtures everyone around her—introduced us with "Do you two know each other?" The answer was no, but we did from that moment forward. There was a spark that just can't be explained.

When I say we've lived life's ups and downs together, I mean it from the bottom of my heart. When Heather went through an awful divorce and had very few people to trust, I was her confidante. I was the one sitting on the phone with her until 1:00 a.m., even though we live on opposite coasts of the United States. That's what real community relationships look like; they transcend geography and time zones when someone you care about needs support.

Sure, the law of propinquity comes into play here. Am I as close to many people in Buffini as I used to be? No. We don't have the built-in mechanism anymore to see each other regularly, and the truth is some relationships are going to drift or are only meant for a season. But then there are people in that community who I still talk to and engage with consistently, and—of course—a long list of ones I know I can call in an instant if needed.

That's the reality of community relationships; they exist on a spectrum. Some evolve into lifelong friendships, others serve their purpose during a specific season, and many fall somewhere in between as connections you can activate when needed. The key is understanding that all of these types of relationships have value, and the foundation you build in the community creates options and opportunities that can last for decades.

The Wrong Way to Build Community

You've all seen them at networking events and community gatherings. They're the ones scanning name tags before making eye contact, qualifying conversations based on job titles, and moving on quickly when someone doesn't seem immediately "useful."

You've watched them work a room like they're collecting trading cards, grabbing business cards, giving their elevator pitch to anyone who will listen, and measuring success by how many contacts they can add to their phone by the end of the night.

You've seen them show up only when they need something. They're absent from community events for months, then suddenly appear when they need something, are launching a business, or are looking for referrals. Their engagement is sporadic and entirely self-serving.

You've witnessed the person who treats every conversation as a transaction. They listen just long enough to determine if you can help them, then either dive into their pitch or politely excuse themselves to find someone more "valuable."

You've observed them join multiple communities simultaneously, spreading themselves so thin that they never really invest deeply in any of them. They're members everywhere but belong nowhere.

This transactional approach to community building isn't just ineffective; it's counterproductive. People can sense when you're more interested in what they can do for you than who they are as a person. It creates an energy that repels rather than attracts, and it often backfires in ways that damage your reputation within the community.

The wrong way to build community is to show up with your hand out, looking for immediate returns on your investment. It's treating every conversation as a means to an end and every relationship as a stepping stone to something better.

The Right Way to Build Community

The right way to build community is to apply the same relational principles we've discussed throughout this book, even with people who might be your colleagues or competitors.

Let me tell you about how I met one of my closest friends, Tara Renze.

When I first joined a community for keynote speakers, one of the bureau agents who reviewed my speaker evaluation said something that stopped me in my tracks. On the evaluation, there was a question that asked them, "What speaker is this person most like?" Their answer: "You remind me of a speaker named Tara Renze."

At that point, I had never met Tara. I didn't even know who she was. So of course, I looked her up. And instantly thought, *Yep. I see it. She's amazing.*

Here's where most people would either do nothing or send a generic connection request. But I knew that real relationships require intentionality. So I followed her. I engaged with her content. I commented meaningfully on her posts. She responded (eventually), and I put my relationship-building skills to work, not by chance, but with clear intention.

I even tried to meet her in Kansas City once, and let's just say the vibe was less "OMG besties" and more "Who is this overly friendly stranger?" But I didn't let that discourage me. Over time, the conversations became more real and more intentional.

Here's what I've learned about relationship building that most people get wrong: They expect immediate reciprocity. When someone doesn't match their energy right away, they assume rejection and retreat. But neutrality isn't rejection—it's often just caution. Some of the strongest relationships I've built started with polite distance, not because the other person didn't like me, but because they were still figuring out if I was genuine.

The key is persistence without pushiness. I kept showing up authentically, engaging with Tara's content meaningfully, and offering value without expecting anything in return. I didn't take her initial coolness personally because I understood something crucial: Trust takes time to build, especially for successful people who've learned to be selective about who gets access to their time and energy.

Most people give up after the first lukewarm response, interpreting professional politeness as personal rejection. But the relationships that transform your life are often the ones that require patience. The slow burn creates deeper trust because it proves your interest isn't superficial or opportunistic.

Then came December. We were both attending an event in Nashville. I let her know I'd be there, and she replied, "I'm excited to finally meet you!" When I arrived and found my table, guess who was already assigned to it? Tara. And guess what else? I may or may not have moved her name tag right next to mine. (When I say I'm intentional, I mean it!)

That day, we finally met in person. And the moment felt easy. Familiar. Like something that had been building for a while. Now? She's one of my closest friends. We talk daily. We cheer each other on. We show up for each other at work and in life.

In fact, not too long ago I boarded a plane on a whim and flew to Kansas City just to surprise her at her book launch party. I wanted her to feel the love, the support, and the celebration she so freely gives to others. The look on her face when she saw me walk in—completely unexpected—was a reminder that the best relationships aren't just convenient; they're intentional. They require showing up when it matters most, not when it's easy.

And that's the beauty of it. A friendship that began with a simple, intentional hello has grown into one of the most meaningful connections in my life.

When You Have to Be Brave to Build Community

Sometimes building community requires courage, the kind that makes your palms sweat and your heart race. The kind that forces you to confront the stories you've been telling yourself about who belongs where and whether you're worthy of a seat at the table.

For years, I had watched Heather Ozur from a distance in our real estate association community. She wasn't just another real estate volunteer; she was part of something I desperately wanted to be part of but felt completely shut out from. Heather belonged to this group of women I quietly admired from across conference rooms and networking events. They were powerful, polished, and always together. They moved through industry events like they owned them, and in many ways they did. They were rising in leadership roles I dreamed of and making the kind of impact I was working toward. They even had a title for themselves: The Fab Five.

But they felt completely unapproachable.

If I'm being brutally honest, I had convinced myself that Heather was a mean girl. It's embarrassing to admit now, but I had created this entire narrative in my head about her and her circle. They seemed so tight-knit, so exclusive, that I assumed they wouldn't want someone like me in their world. When I saw them laughing together at events, I told myself they were probably talking about people like me—the ones on the outside looking in. When they walked past me in hotel lobbies without stopping to chat, I convinced myself it was intentional exclusion rather than just busy people focused on their own conversations.

I had built walls around them in my mind and then resented them for the barriers I had created.

The truth is I was intimidated. They represented everything I was working toward, and my own insecurities made me assume they saw me as competition rather than a potential friend. It was easier to label them as mean girls than to admit I was scared they might not think I was good enough to be part of their circle.

One thing you need to know about me: I don't eat alone very well. There's something about sitting by myself in a restaurant, especially in an unfamiliar city, that makes me feel exposed and lonely. Now fast-forward: As a keynote speaker who travels alone a ton, I am very used to eating by myself, but back to the story.

I was preparing to travel to Chicago for a new advisory group I'd been invited to join. This was a real honor that I was both excited and nervous about. I knew I needed to find someone to have dinner with the night before the event started.

I pulled up the attendee list and scrolled through the names to see who else would be there. That's when I spotted my friend Leslie's name; she was someone I thought would be a safe bet for company. We had built a relationship already, and I always enjoyed her presence. I reached out to her, asking if she wanted to get together for dinner. But she was busy with plans to meet up with some college friends.

I sat at home the day before my flight, staring at my phone, dreading the thought of spending my first evening in Chicago wandering around alone, looking for a place to eat. That's when I pulled up the attendee list again, trying to see who else would be there, wondering if I had the courage to reach out to anyone else.

And then I saw Heather's name flashing out at me.

My heart started racing. My palms actually got sweaty. This was the woman I had labeled as unapproachable; she was part of a group I had convinced myself didn't want anything to do with me. But I was faced with a choice: Spend the evening alone or take a chance on being rejected by someone who might actually be kinder than I had imagined.

I must have typed and deleted that message ten times. *What if she ignores me? What if she says no in a way that confirms all my fears about not belonging? What if this is the moment that prove I really am on the outside of this community I so desperately want to be part of?*

But finally, I thought, *Well, the worst thing she can say is no. And I'm already gonna be alone, so how much worse could it get?*

I sent the message, probably overthinking every word: "Hey! I know this is last minute, but I'm wondering if you'd like to grab dinner tomorrow night before everything kicks off?"

I immediately regretted it. Too casual? Too presumptuous? Should I have been more formal? Less formal? I was spiraling in that special way that happens when you realize you've just made yourself vulnerable to someone whose opinion matters to you.

Her response came back almost immediately, way faster than I expected: "ABSOLUTELY! You should join my friend Rebecca and me for dinner. We'd love to have you!"

I stared at that message, reading it three times to make sure I wasn't misunderstanding. Not only was she saying yes, but she was also including me in plans she already had with someone else. She was welcoming me into her circle, the very circle I had convinced myself was impenetrable.

That dinner in Chicago was a revelation. Heather wasn't mean at all; she was warm, funny, and genuinely interested in getting to know me. Rebecca was equally welcoming, and the three of us talked for hours about business, life, dreams, and challenges. They asked about my goals, shared their own struggles, and treated me like I belonged at that table from the very first moment I sat down.

What I discovered that night is that the barriers I thought existed were entirely in my own mind. These women weren't exclusive because they didn't want others around; they were close because they had done the work of building genuine relationships with each other. And they were more than happy to extend that warmth to someone who was brave enough to ask for it.

Fast-forward ten years later, and that dinner sparked one of the most important relationships in my life, not just with Heather, but with Rebecca too. These women have become some of my closest friends, my business advisors, my cheerleaders, and my truth tellers. They've supported me through career transitions, celebrated my wins, and been there through personal challenges. What started as a desperate attempt to avoid eating alone became the foundation for friendships that have shaped both my business and my life.

The lesson I learned that night in Chicago has stuck with me through every community I've joined since: Sometimes the people we think are "mean girls" or "unapproachable" are actually just waiting for someone to be brave enough to reach out. Sometimes the walls we see are just shadows cast by our own insecurities and assumptions.

Heather wasn't mean; I had created that story in my head because it felt safer to assume rejection than to risk finding out I might actually belong. I had let my own fears and limiting beliefs keep me from connections that were right there, waiting to be made.

Building community sometimes means getting uncomfortable, reaching across perceived barriers, and discovering that the invitation to belong might be closer than we think. It means being willing to challenge the stories we tell ourselves about who wants us around and who doesn't.

Most importantly, it means being brave enough to send the message, make the call, or walk across the room—even when your palms are sweaty and your heart is racing. Because on the other side of that courage might be exactly the community you've been looking for all along.

When people ask me, "How do you build community wherever you go?" my answer is simple: I just focus on humans and relationships, and the rest just happens on its own.

When I joined the speaking community in March 2024, for example, I knew absolutely no one. I had one person who introduced me to the community, but they weren't even a part of it themselves. I joined, I immersed myself in it, and I treated people like humans. I built relationships, used my Relationship Operating System, and did my thing.

Fast-forward to December 2024, just nine months later, at their annual "Un-Gala," I was presented with a speakers' community award for members who uphold their core values, and I received "With a Little Help from My Friends," which recognizes the community member who is always there for everyone, creating community wherever they go.

To say I was honored is an understatement. But here's what that award really represents: It's proof that authentic relationship building works, regardless of the setting. When you show up genuinely, invest in others consistently, and focus on adding value rather than extracting it, community naturally forms around you.

The Compound Effect of Community Investment

Here's what most people don't understand about community building: The returns are rarely immediate, but they're almost always exponential. Show up, do the work, and build the relationships, and opportunities will happen.

I built my real estate business in community. In 2008, one of the lowest points of the real estate market during the Great Recession, 68 percent of our business that year came from referrals from agents I met in Buffini & Company, both in and out of California. When the market was at its worst, the relationships I had invested in became our lifeline.

Or take the power of the speaking community I've mentioned previously, which has exponentially fast-tracked my speaking career. There are countless opportunities, referrals, and new relationships that have all transcended to actual bookings on my calendar. None of that happens by accident. It happens because I showed up consistently, contributed meaningfully, and invested genuinely in the success of others.

The key is that these relationships weren't built with those outcomes in mind. They were built through genuine care, consistent support, and authentic investment in others' success.

Communities become powerful when you approach them as ecosystems rather than hunting grounds. An ecosystem is a network of interconnected relationships where everyone benefits from the success of others.

In my speaking community, I celebrate when other speakers get great gigs because I know their success elevates the entire industry. I make introductions between speakers and event planners, between authors and publishers, and between coaches and potential clients, not because I expect immediate reciprocity, but because I understand that a thriving ecosystem benefits everyone.

The Ecosystem Approach

This ecosystem approach has created opportunities I never could have imagined. Doors have opened, introductions have been made, and partnerships have formed, all because I focused on contributing to the community rather than just extracting from it.

Just like individual relationships, community relationships require intentionality and systems. I maintain a simple but effective approach:

- Before every event or meeting, I ask myself a simple question: *How can I add value to this gathering?* Sometimes that means bringing a helpful resource. Other times, it's making a strategic introduction or simply being the person who remembers to celebrate others' wins.

- After every community interaction, I make it a point to follow up with at least three people—not to sell, but to continue a conversation, share a resource I promised, or just let them know I enjoyed meeting them. That small follow-through often leads to the most meaningful connections.
- I track community relationships the same way I track client ones. I note important details, set reminders to reconnect, and look for ways to support their goals over time. Long-term relationships aren't built by accident. They're built by intention.
- And one of my favorite connection habits: I make dinner reservations ahead of events. I always book a few extra spots and invite others along—especially those who seem new or left out. That person standing alone at the networking mixer? They're coming with me. Some of my closest professional relationships started that way: one extra chair at a table, one intentional invite, one moment of inclusion that made all the difference.

Because that's the thing about community—it's not built in one moment. It's built in the little things that add up over time. And when you keep showing up that way, community doesn't just grow. It becomes part of your legacy.

When Community Becomes Legacy

The most powerful aspect of community building is how it extends your impact far beyond your individual reach. When you invest genuinely in a community, you're not just building relationships; you're building a legacy.

The agents I mentored in my real estate community are now mentoring others. The speakers I've supported in my speaking community are now opening doors for newer speakers. The leaders I've worked alongside in professional organizations are now creating opportunities for the next generation of leaders.

This is the true power of community: It multiplies your influence by creating a network of people who carry your values, your approach, and your commitment to excellence into their own circles of influence.

Here's something I've learned through years of community involvement: The right communities don't just provide opportunities; they provide accountability, inspiration, and support that elevate every aspect of your professional life.

When you're surrounded by people who share your commitment to excellence, who celebrate your successes and support you through challenges, and who challenge you to grow and hold you accountable to your goals, you become a better version of yourself.

The communities I've been part of haven't just given me business opportunities. They've given me lifelong friendships, professional partnerships, and a network of people who genuinely care about my success and whom I genuinely care about supporting.

Your Community Strategy: Five Steps to Authentic Connection

As you think about building your own community network, here's a practical framework that has guided my approach across every community I've joined:

1. **Choose with intention.** Find communities aligned with your values and goals, not just where you think you "should" be.

Look for places where you genuinely share the mission, where the people inspire you, and where you're excited about the journey, not just the destination. Start by identifying what matters most to you. Industry associations and professional groups are obvious choices, but don't overlook alumni networks, hobby-based communities, or cause-specific organizations where shared values create stronger bonds than pure networking. The best communities often aren't the largest or most prestigious.

2. **Show up consistently.** Attend regularly and engage meaningfully, not just when you need something or when it's convenient. True community building happens in the consistent moments between the big events, in the follow-up conversations and the ongoing support you provide to others.
3. **Contribute before you extract.** Add value first and build relationships genuinely; always ask, "How can I help?" before wondering, *What can I get?* Look for ways to support others' goals, make introductions, share resources, and celebrate wins before you ever need to ask for anything in return.
4. **Invest in systems.** Follow up intentionally, track meaningful relationships, and remember the details that matter to people. Use the same systematic approach for community relationships that you would for your most important business relationships, because that's exactly what they can become.
5. **Think long-term.** Focus on building foundations rather than seeking immediate returns, understanding that the best community relationships compound over years, not months. Plant seeds without knowing exactly when or how they'll bloom, trusting that authentic investment always creates unexpected opportunities.

Remember that authenticity always wins. The communities you build today will shape the opportunities you have tomorrow, but more importantly, they'll shape the person you become and the legacy you leave. Because in the end, success isn't just about what you achieve; it's about what you make possible for others along the way.

The power of community lies not in what you can take from it but in what you choose to give to it. And when you give generously, consistently, and authentically, the returns in relationships, opportunities, and impact will exceed anything you could have imagined.

CHAPTER 14

The Legacy You Leave— Living in the Dash

On every tombstone there are two dates separated by a simple dash. The first date marks when we arrived in this world. The second marks when we left. But it's that small dash between them that tells the real story—the story of how we lived, who we loved, and what we left behind.

I don't believe your legacy is always measured in the accumulation of wealth or the height of your achievements. I believe it's measured in the depth of your relationships and the ripple effects they create long after you're gone. Because here's the truth: Relationships don't die with us. They live on, multiply, and continue to create impact through the networks we've built and the lives we've touched.

When you invest in relationships with intention, trust, and care, you're not just building connections; you're creating a living legacy. Each relationship becomes a seed that grows into something far greater than the original investment.

That twenty-year-old colleague you mentored five years ago—the one who once stumbled through her first client call and leaned on you to polish her reports—now leads her own team. She's mentoring interns with the same patience you once showed her, and from afar, it's fulfilling to watch her confidence and influence grow.

The client you served with excellence—the one you stayed late to help during a chaotic project—still talks about your reliability. Today, they're a senior leader who now recommends you to others, opening doors you never expected.

And that friend you supported through a difficult season? They've become the one who shows up for others in their hardest moments, carrying forward the same compassion you once offered them.

This is the compound effect of human connection. It multiplies exponentially, creating ripples that extend far beyond what we can see or measure. Every genuine relationship you build becomes part of a network that continues to grow and create value long after the initial connection.

When One Conversation Changes Everything

Seventeen years ago, my husband, Harold, was coaching our son's travel baseball team, the Lakewood Lugnuts. It was a fun team filled with families we'd known for years—the kind of relationships that develop naturally when you're spending every weekend together on baseball fields across Southern California. Remember that law of propinquity? Relationships form through repeated exposure and shared experiences. Those tournament weekends, team dinners, and hours in the stands created the perfect conditions for deep, lasting connections to develop naturally.

One day, Harold came home excited about a new player he'd added to the team: Nick Reeser. I had no idea who Nick was or anything about his family. At that time, I was teaching dance and often missed Saturday morning games, rushing over as soon as my classes ended.

But this particular weekend, Harold was adamant that I come to the game immediately after teaching. He had fallen in love with Nick as a player—and so had our son. We were getting ready to take our team to a big tournament in Colorado, a ten-day trip where families would rent houses together. It was a big deal, a significant investment of time and money.

Harold had one request for me: "I need you to convince Nick's mom to let him come to Colorado with us."

So I did what I do—I went to build a relationship.

I remember walking to the dugout and asking Harold, "Where is the mom?" He pointed to a chair where a woman with blonde hair and sunglasses sat doing what all good baseball moms do: She was watching her son intently.

I approached her and introduced myself. I started with small talk and relatability—the universal experiences of baseball parents, the joys and anxieties of watching your kid play, and the logistics of travel ball life. Then I naturally transitioned the conversation to getting to know her and her family.

We talked the entire rest of the game. Not about the Colorado trip at first—about life, about our kids, about our work. She was an elementary school teacher. We talked about the things that matter to parents trying to do right by their children, the challenges of balancing work and family, and the dreams we had for our sons.

By the end of the conversation, she said yes to Colorado.

But more importantly, that conversation started something neither of us expected. That woman's name is Katrina, and seventeen years later, she's my best friend.

What started as a mission to convince a stranger to trust us with her son became one of the most important relationships in my life. But it didn't happen overnight. It was built over time, through consistent investment, genuine care, and the kind of trust that develops when you show up for someone again and again.

You never know where a relationship is going to lead you. What seems like a simple conversation at a baseball game can become a friendship that transforms your life. What appears to be a brief encounter can evolve into decades of shared experiences, mutual support, and genuine love.

This story illustrates something crucial that often gets lost when we talk about relationship building: While the strategies and mindsets in this book will absolutely transform your professional circles, their most meaningful impact often unfolds in spaces that have nothing to do with your career.

My friendship with Katrina didn't advance my business or open professional doors. It gave me something far more valuable—a person who knows my heart, who I can call at 2:00 a.m. when life feels heavy, who celebrates my wins without agenda, and who shows up in my hardest moments without hesitation.

Relationships like this remind us that the same principles that elevate your career—authentic curiosity, consistent care, seeing people as whole humans—can create profound richness in every area of life. The colleague who becomes a lifelong friend. The neighbor who becomes family. The chance encounter that grows into decades of mutual support.

Professional relationships may open doors, but personal ones built with the same intentionality sustain your soul. When you cultivate authentic connections across every sphere—work, community, friendship—you create a network of care that carries you through any challenge and magnifies every joy.

The principles are universal. The outcomes are limitless. And the most treasured relationships often bloom in the most unexpected places.

Baseball eventually ended for our boys, but our friendship didn't. It deepened. Katrina and I have been there through each other's families' highest highs and our lowest lows. We've celebrated each other's victories and picked each other up when we've been down. We've been through health challenges together—I've taken her to a life-changing surgery, and she's sat with me through my own difficult health moments. We've learned to be honest and transparent with each other, even when it's hard—especially when it's hard.

She's the friend I call when I need honest advice, genuine support, or just someone who truly knows me. She's also the friend who will tell me the truth when I need to hear it, even if it's not what I want to hear. That's what real friendship looks like—it's built on trust deep enough to handle both celebration and struggle, both encouragement and accountability.

This is what the compound effect of relationships looks like. What Harold saw as a simple request—"Convince this mom to let her son come to Colorado"—became a relationship that has enriched my life for nearly two decades. The initial investment of one genuine conversation has paid dividends in ways I never could have imagined.

Looking back, that moment at the baseball field required a small act of courage—not because I had to "be authentic," but because I had to be myself with a complete stranger. I had to approach someone I didn't know and trust that genuine conversation would be enough. I had to believe that if I simply showed up as who I really was and shared honestly about our family and our love for baseball, she would feel comfortable entrusting her son to us for ten days.

There was no script, no strategy. Just one parent talking to another parent about the things that matter most—our kids, our hopes for them, and our desire to give them experiences that would shape them in positive ways.

But that one moment of simply being real created something that has lasted far beyond that Colorado tournament, far beyond our sons' baseball careers, and far beyond the context that brought us together.

This is the power of approaching every interaction as an opportunity to build something real. You never know which conversation will change your life, which relationship will become central to your story, or which moment of authentic connection will create decades of friendship.

My relationship with Katrina started as "Nick's mom who needs convincing." Today, she's family. That transformation didn't happen because of any grand gesture or dramatic moment. It happened because of consistent, authentic relationship building over time—through seasons of joy and seasons of challenge, through moments when it was easy to show up and moments when it was hard.

And it all started with one conversation that I could have approached transactionally but chose to approach relationally instead. That choice—to see every interaction as an opportunity to connect genuinely with another human being—has shaped not just my business success but also my life satisfaction. Because in the end, relationships aren't just your competitive advantage in business. They're your advantage in life.

What Most People Get Wrong About Legacy

Most people think legacy is about what you leave behind: your accomplishments, your bank account, and the plaques on your wall. But that's not legacy; that's history. True legacy is about what continues forward: the people you've influenced, the connections you've facilitated, and the trust you've built that others carry into their own relationships.

Your credentials document what you did. A legacy demonstrates what you made possible for others.

The difference is profound. Your achievements are finite—they happened in a specific time and place, and then they're done. But your relationships are infinite—they continue to create new possibilities, new connections, and new opportunities long after you're no longer part of the equation.

Think about the people who have had the greatest impact on your life. Chances are it wasn't because of their impressive credentials or their list of accomplishments. It was because of how they made you feel, how they invested in you, and how they opened doors or provided opportunities that changed your trajectory. That's relational legacy in action.

Here's what makes relational legacy so powerful: It doesn't just impact the people you directly connect with. When you invest deeply in someone, you're also investing in everyone they will influence in the future. When you help someone succeed, you're contributing to all the people they'll help succeed. When you build trust with one person, you're potentially building credibility with their entire network.

This is why some people seem to have opportunities constantly flowing their way while others struggle to get noticed despite impressive qualifications. It's not about what they know or what they've done—it's about who trusts them and who's willing to vouch for them.

The most successful people understand this intuitively. They know that investing in relationships isn't just good business practice—it's legacy building. Every authentic connection they make, every person they genuinely help, and every moment they choose relationship over transaction, they're writing a story that will continue long after they're gone.

Let me share a story that perfectly illustrates this principle—the story of my son, Chris.

Chris was born with something special: a natural charisma and an instinct to see people, really see them, and connect with them as human beings. In middle school, while other kids were focused on fitting in with the popular crowd, Chris joined Best Buddies, a program that paired students with special needs kids. But for Chris, these weren't charity cases; they were his best friends. This wasn't performative kindness; it was just who he was.

This character trait continued into high school, where Chris excelled both on the baseball field, earning recognition as one of the top players in the nation, and in the hallways, where he was known as the guy who knew everyone's name and made everyone feel valued. His teammates, coaches, teachers, and custodial staff—everyone felt seen by Chris.

Chris was drafted in the 2015 MLB draft as the fifty-second pick overall to the Tampa Bay Rays. From his first day in professional baseball, he did the same thing he'd always done: He treated people like humans, not roles.

But Chris's playing career took an unexpected turn. Like many promising young athletes, his journey was plagued with injuries and setbacks. Anyone familiar with minor league baseball knows that once the injury bug hits, recovery is incredibly difficult. Every day on the disabled list is another day someone else is taking your spot.

Where others might have seen these setbacks as career-ending obstacles, Chris saw them as relationship-building opportunities. While rehabbing in training rooms, he wasn't just focused on getting his body back—he was building friendships with trainers, physical therapists, and medical staff. When he stayed behind at spring training for extended rehab, he connected with year-round staff, the facilities crew, and other players going through similar struggles.

While other players were laser-focused on stats and climbing the ladder, Chris understood something different: It wasn't just about how many home runs he could hit. It was about the people and how he showed up for them.

Eventually, the injuries caught up, and at twenty-five, Chris retired from professional baseball. For many, this would have felt like the end of a dream. For Chris, it was the beginning of something bigger.

Almost immediately, Chris became an MLB-certified player agent. This career pivot shocked people. How does a recently retired player with no agent experience suddenly enter one of the most competitive industries in sports?

Chris didn't walk into this career empty-handed. He walked in with a decade of relationships forged in trust—with front-office executives and clubhouse staff, trainers and equipment managers, grounds crew and mascots. People who knew him liked him and respected how he'd handled both success and adversity.

The results speak for themselves: By age twenty-seven, Chris had two World Series champions under his representation. To put this in perspective, most agents spend decades building their client base. Many never represent a single major league player, let alone World Series champions.

Recently, he was offered a role at Creative Artists Agency (CAA)—the number one agency in the world. Not because of his résumé or credentials, but because they saw how he was doing it. "We want to know what you know," they told him. "We want to understand how you build trust like that."

In an industry where many agents succeed through aggressive tactics, Chris proved there's a better way. His approach wasn't about selling; it was about serving. It wasn't about convincing people to trust him; it was about being trustworthy.

Now, Chris absolutely did this on his own through his character and effort. But here's what makes this story meaningful to me: Chris grew up watching his parents build our business the exact same way—through relationships, not transactions. He inherited something far more valuable than money: a blueprint for creating success through authentic connection.

This is what legacy really looks like. When the next generation doesn't just hear about your values but sees them lived out consistently over time.

Building Networks That Outlast You

The relationships you build don't exist in isolation. They connect to form networks, and those networks become part of your lasting legacy. When you introduce two people who go on to create something meaningful together, you've created a connection that lives beyond you. When you invest in someone's development and they go on to develop others, you've started a chain reaction that can span generations.

Think about the most influential people in your life. Now think about how they've influenced others. The teacher who believed in you didn't just impact your life—they impacted everyone you've gone on to influence. The mentor who guided you didn't just change your trajectory—they changed the trajectory of everyone you've mentored since.

This is how legacies are truly built—through the multiplication of relationships and the compound effect of human connection.

Your relational legacy extends far beyond your professional network. The way you build relationships within your family creates patterns that can last for generations. The intentionality you bring to your friendships models what healthy connection looks like. The way you engage with your community creates ripples that touch lives you may never know about.

When you choose to be the person who remembers birthdays, who checks in during difficult times, who celebrates others' successes with genuine joy—you're creating a standard of relationship that others will carry forward. You're building a legacy of care, intention, and authentic connection.

Take a moment and picture the scene with me. You're looking down at your own memorial service. The venue your family chose: What does it look like? Is it filled to capacity, or are there empty chairs scattered throughout? Listen closely. What are people saying as they gather? Are they trading heartfelt stories about how you showed up for them—or polite small talk because they barely knew you beyond your professional role?

Notice who's there. Are they just colleagues fulfilling an obligation or people whose lives you truly impacted? Look for the unexpected faces. The assistant you mentored twenty years ago who drove three hours to be there, the client who became a dear friend, the neighbor whose family you helped through a crisis.

Now listen to the eulogies. What stories are being told? Are they about titles and achievements, or are they about the time you remembered someone's daughter's graduation, the way you showed up during their divorce, or the connection you made that changed their career?

Linger at the reception afterward. Are people staying to share memories, or are they quietly slipping out? Do you see clusters of people who met through you—still connected because of a bond you helped form years ago?

Here's your exercise: Write down five people you hope would speak at your funeral. Not because they should, but because they would *want* to. What story would each of them tell to capture the impact you had on their life?

Then ask the harder question: Based on how you're showing up today, would those stories exist? Would those people be there?

This isn't meant to be morbid; it's meant to be motivating. Your funeral is a future event you can shape, day by day, through the relationships you choose to build and nurture. Every authentic conversation, every moment you choose connection over convenience, every act of generosity—you're writing the stories that will one day be told in that room.

The beautiful truth is this: You get to decide what that room looks like. Whether your legacy is measured in transactions or in transformations, in achievements or in relationships. And if you build with intention, love, and care, your legacy will live on in every story they share.

The Systematic Approach to Legacy Building

Building a lasting relational legacy doesn't happen by accident. It requires the same intentional systems and practices we've discussed throughout this book:

- **The Daily Investment:** Make someone's day, every day. These small, consistent investments compound over time to create extraordinary relationship dividends.
- **The Long-Term View:** Remember that some relationships may not pay dividends for years, but when they do, the return is often exponentially greater than the original investment.
- **The Network Effect:** Actively look for ways to connect others in your network. When you become known as a connector, you multiply your relational impact.
- **The Value-First Approach:** Always lead with generosity. Ask what you can offer before you ask for anything in return.

The ultimate measure of your relational legacy is not just who you've influenced, but who those people go on to influence. When you invest in developing others' relationship skills, when you model authentic connection, when you create opportunities for others to build their own networks—you're ensuring that your legacy multiplies.

The best relationship builders don't just create strong networks; they create other relationship builders. They pass on the skills, the mindset, and the systems that make authentic connection possible.

Your dash—that space between your birth date and your death date—is still being written. Every interaction, every relationship, and every moment of authentic connection is adding to the legacy you'll leave behind.

But here's what makes this truly exciting: Your legacy doesn't end with your dash. The relationships you build, the networks you create, and the people you influence—they all continue to grow and create impact long after you're gone.

The colleague you mentor today becomes the leader who changes an industry tomorrow. The client you serve with excellence becomes the advocate who opens doors for years to come. The friend you support through difficulty becomes the person who supports countless others in their time of need.

This is the true power of relational legacy: It's not about what you accomplish in your lifetime, but about what you make possible for others to accomplish in theirs.

Your Legacy Starts Today

The beautiful thing about legacy is that it's not something you build at the end of your life; it's something you're building every day. Every relationship you invest in, every person you lift up, and every connection you facilitate is adding to the legacy you'll leave behind.

Your funeral may be decades away, but the relationships that will fill it are being built today. The network effects that will continue long after you're gone are being created right now, in this moment, with every person you choose to see, value, and authentically connect with.

The question isn't whether you'll leave a legacy—we all leave one. The question is, What kind of legacy will it be?

Will it be a legacy of authentic connection, of lives touched and changed, of networks that continue to create value long after you're gone? Will it be a legacy of intentional relationship building, of trust earned and maintained, of doors opened for others?

The choice is yours, and it starts with your next interaction. Here's the truth that will outlast every trend, every technology, and every business strategy: Relationships are the only currency that appreciates forever.

While everything else depreciates—your skills become outdated, your knowledge becomes obsolete, your achievements fade into history—the relationships you build with intention, trust, and care compound infinitely. They create ripple effects that touch lives you'll never meet, open doors you never knew existed, and solve problems you never imagined.

Chris's story isn't just about one young man's success. It's about the power of living with relational intention every single day. It's about understanding that the person you help today might become the person who changes your life tomorrow. It's about recognizing that every interaction is an investment in a future you can't yet see.

You don't need a fancy title, an impressive résumé, or years of experience to start building your relational legacy. You just need to see people—really see them—and treat them like they matter. Because they do.

The janitor you acknowledge by name today might become the CEO who remembers your kindness. The colleague you mentor might become the leader who opens the door to your next opportunity. The client you serve with excellence might become the advocate who transforms your career. The friend you support through their darkest hour might become the person who celebrates your greatest triumph.

This is the mathematics of relationship building: small, consistent investments of authentic care create exponential returns that compound across generations.

Your funeral will be filled with relationships, not résumés. Your legacy will be measured in lives touched, not dollars accumulated. Your impact will be remembered in the people you lifted up, not the positions you climbed to.

The dash between your dates, that small line that represents your entire existence, is being written right now. Every conversation, every act of kindness, and every moment of authentic connection is adding to the story that will outlive you.

But here's what makes this truly extraordinary: Your story doesn't end with your dash. The relationships you build, the trust you earn, the lives you touch—they all continue to create impact long after you're gone. They become part of other people's stories, other people's successes, and other people's legacies.

When you build relationships with intention, trust, and care, doors open that no amount of hustle can unlock. But more importantly, you create a legacy that lives on through every person you've touched, every connection you've facilitated, and every life you've made better through the power of authentic human connection.

Your dash is still being written. Make it count.

Make it relational.

Make it matter.

The world is waiting for the relationships only you can build.

ACKNOWLEDGMENTS

First, to my husband, Harold, my partner in every sense of the word—this book is as much yours as it is mine. Who would have thought two teenagers who became parents at eighteen and married shortly after would build this story together? Twenty-eight years later, you're still my best friend and living proof that the strongest relationships aren't built on perfect timing or ideal circumstances but on choosing each other every single day.

Thank you for being by my side through every chapter of our story—for being my business partner when I needed support, my life partner when I needed strength, my lover when I needed passion, and my confidant when I needed truth. You've been my soulmate through the planned moments and the unexpected ones, through the dreams we chased and the challenges we never saw coming. You are the relationship I am most proud of.

To our son, Chris—you inspire me daily with your grit, your heart, and the way you've built your own path through both talent and the relationships you've nurtured along the way. Watching you chase your dreams and succeed is one of my life's greatest joys.

To our daughter, Mandy—you are kind, steady, and quietly strong. You don't let just anyone into your world, and that's one of the things I most admire about you. You've shown me what it looks like to have a powerful relationship with yourself, one rooted in quiet confidence and authenticity. You remind me that you don't have to be the loudest voice in the room to make the deepest impact. Your way of moving through the world teaches me daily that self-trust is one of the most beautiful forms of strength.

This book exists because of the foundation we've built as a family. Each of you has shaped who I am, stretched what I believe is possible, and given me the courage to put these words into the world. Everything I write about relationships is real because I've lived it first with you.

ABOUT THE AUTHOR

Barb Betts is a keynote speaker, entrepreneur, and CEO with more than twenty years of experience showing people that relationships aren't just part of business—they *are* the business. She has built multimillion-dollar companies and helped sales teams, leaders, and organizations transform their performance by shifting from chasing transactions to building authentic, trust-driven connections.

She is the host of the award-winning podcast *Relationships Are Your Superpower®* and has shared the stage at premier events for organizations like Louis Vuitton Moët Hennessy (LVMH), Fidelity National, American Pacific Mortgage, and the National Association of REALTORS® Annual Conference. Her contagious energy and actionable strategies leave audiences inspired and equipped with a clear plan to grow referrals, deepen loyalty, and build businesses that last.

For Barb, relationships aren't an abstract idea—they're a measurable asset that drives revenue, influence, and impact. Her signature methodology proves that when you invest in authentic connections, success becomes easier, more sustainable, and far more fulfilling.

When she's not speaking or mentoring other business owners, Barb can be found in Southern California with her husband and two amazing kids, living the very principles she teaches: prioritizing relationships, creating memories, and building a meaningful legacy.